D0458456

THE SCIENCE OF SELF-REALIZATION

Roy Eugene Davis has taught these spiritual growth processes in North American, Japan, West Africa, Brazil, Europe, and India. He was ordained by Paramahansa Yogananda in 1951.

The international headquarters of Center for Spiritual Awareness is located in the northeast Georgia mountains, ninety miles from Atlanta. Facilities include the offices and publishing department, a meeting hall and dining room, the Shrine of All Faiths Meditation Temple, two libraries, guest houses, and a book store. Meditation retreats are offered from early spring until late autumn.

For a free information packet and book list, contact:

Center for Spiritual Awareness
Post Office Box 7
Lakemont, Georgia 30552-0001

Telephone 706-782-4723 weekdays 8 a.m. to 3 p.m.
Fax 706-782-4560
E-mail: csainc@csa-davis.org
Internet Web Site: www.csa-davis.org

The Science of Self-Realization

A Guide to Spiritual Practice in the Kriya Yoga Tradition

Patanjali's Yoga-Sutras
(new translation, with commentary)

Roy Eugene Davis
A direct disciple of Paramahansa Yogananda

CSA Press / Lakemont, Georgia

ISBN 0-87707-292-2

CSA Press
P. O. Box 7
Lakemont, Georgia 30552-0001

Tel: 706-782-4723
Fax: 706-782-4560
e-mail: csainc@csa-davis.org
Web Site: www.csa-davis.org

CSA Press is the publishing department
of Center for Spiritual Awareness.

PRINTED IN THE UNITED STATES OF AMERICA

INVOCATION

Reverently open your mind and your heart
(the essence of your being) to the Infinite.

Acknowledge:

The reality of God within and around you.
The saints and sages of all enlightenment traditions.
The innate, divine nature of every person.
That all knowledge of the unbounded field of
Infinite Consciousness is within you.

Affirm:

May I be steadfast on my spiritual path as
I know it to be and as it is revealed to me.
May I be permanently established in conscious
realization of my relationship with the Infinite.
May everyone be spiritually enlightened.

Books By The Author

Seven Lessons in Conscious Living
The Science of God-Realization
Satisfying Our Innate Desire to Know God
The Self-Revealed Knowledge That Liberates the Spirit
A Master Guide to Meditation
The Eternal Way (Inner Meaning of the Bhagavad Gita)
The Spiritual Basis of Real Prosperity
Life Surrendered In God
The Book of Life
Living in God
An Easy Guide to Ayurveda

Some of Mr. Davis books are published in India by:
Motilal Banarsidass
40 U.A., Bungalow Road, Jawahar Nagar
Delhi 110 007
Tel: 2385-1985   Fax: 011-2385-0689
e-mail: mlbd@vsnl.com   Web site: www.mlbd.com

And at Motilal Banarsidass bookstores in Delhi, Varanasi,
Patna, Kolkata, Chennai, Bangalore, Pune, and Mumbai.

Contents

Introduction   9

PART ONE
Chapter One
Samadhi
Superconscious States and How to Experience Them   13

Chapter Two
Kriya Yoga
Intensive Spiritual Practice   30

Chapter Three
Siddhis
Exceptional Powers of Perception and Extraordinary Abilities   49

Chapter Four
Liberation of Consciousness
The Culmination of Right Practice   66

PART TWO
Chapter Five
The Shandilya Upanishad   79

Chapter Six
The Inner Meaning of the Bhagavad Gita   98

PART THREE
Chapter Seven
Meditation Techniques and Routines
for All Levels of Practice   113

Chapter Eight
Answers to Questions About the Spiritual Path   121

Glossary   131

Introduction

The philosphical principles and spiritual practices described in the yoga-sutras were known for at least three thousand years before Patanjali wrote about them two thousand years ago.

Sutras are concisely presented "threads" of concepts and teachings of a theme which are to be contemplated until their meaning is intellectually and intuitively comprehended.

A practitioner of yoga should know the ultimate purpose of practice to be complete transcendence of ordinary states of consciousness and the superficial values associated with them. The thinking and endeavors of one who aspires to be Self-realized must be both rational and intentional. Practice that is adapted to one's psychological temperament, capacity to learn, and ability to apply what is learned makes the body, mind, and awareness receptive to transcendent realizations.

An intellectual grasp of philosophical concepts should be acquired. A practitioner of yoga must be a dedicated disciple (learner). If the capacity to learn and to practice what is learned is absent, involvement with these processes will be of little value.

A truth seeker should know:

1. That one supreme Consciousness exists.
2. The processes that produced and maintain the cosmos.
3. Why and how souls became involved with nature.
4. How psychological transformation can be accomplished, how the brain and nervous system can be refined, and how spiritual growth that allows Self- and God-realization to be actualized can be quickened.

This new commentary on the yoga-sutras represents my current understanding and provides information that will enable sincerely resolved truth seekers to experience the fulfillment of their innate desire to be Self-realized. The word *science* is included in the title to emphasize the importance of attentive examination, comprehension, and experimental investigation of the concepts and processes that are described and explained.

Read the entire text, including the glossary, to acquire an overview. Then start with chapter one of the yoga-sutras and on a regular schedule read a sutra, or few sutras of a theme, and my commentary. Contemplate the meaning of what is read until the concepts and practices are understood.

I have provided a brief commentary on the sutras. As your understanding improves, you will have your own insights and be able to use what is learned to enhance your overall well-being and improve your practice of meditation.

When I was with my guru, Paramahansa Yogananda, in the early 1950s, I learned from him the principles and meditation methods of the kriya yoga tradition. When he ordained me, he said, "Teach as I have taught. The same God that is in me, is in you. What I have done, you should do." Since then, I have consistently adhered to this path and have taught many others, who were receptive to learning, how to awaken through the stages of spiritual growth.

Roy Eugene Davis

Lakemont, Georgia
Summer, 2004

Note: While reading, if a word or concept is not understood, refer to the glossary in the back of the book.

PART ONE

Patanjali's Yoga-Sutras

CHAPTER ONE

Samadhi

Superconscious States and How to Experience Them

1. Now, instruction in yoga, in accord with an established tradition, begins.

The word *now* indicates an auspicious (favorable) time for this information to be taught to sincere truth seekers who are receptive to learning.

In this text, *yoga* usually means samadhi: "the bringing together completely" of one's attention and awareness with an object of contemplation. Superconscious samadhi is superior to ordinary, blurred and fragmented, states of consciousness.

Reference to an established tradition indicates that what is described is useful knowledge that was known by others.

2. Samadhi is experienced when fluctuations and changes in the meditator's awareness are restrained and pacified.

This sutra (Sanskrit, *yoga-chitta-vritti-nirodha*) describes the specific means by which the ultimate aim of practice is to be realized. Samadhi results when movements and changes (*vrittis*) in individualized consciousness (*chitta*) are weakened, pacified, and become dormant (*nirodha*).

3. The seer then consciously abides in its own nature [essence].

The *seer* is the Self-identity of the meditator that perceives what is observed or experienced. When the wavelike changes and transformations that ordinarily occur in the mind and awareness cease, Self-realization (conscious experience along with knowledge of one's essence of being) prevails.

4. At other times, one is inclined to identify with the changes and transformations that occur in the mind and awareness.

A meditator may enjoy a clear superconscious state while attention is internalized and be inclined to again be attracted to, and to identify with, modifying influences that arise in the mind and awareness after meditation has been practiced.

When Self-realization is stable, the contents of the mind and awareness can be viewed with objectivity.

5. Mental modifications are fivefold. They may cause pain or pleasure according to prevailing circumstances that allow their effects to be actualized.

They may have potential to cause pain, be impure, and be restrictive; or do not cause pain, are pure, and do not restrict our powers of perception or ability to function.

6. The five kinds of transformation that modify mind and awareness are 1) the processes that occur when valid knowledge is acquired; 2) illusion; 3) delusions; 4) sleep; and 5) memory.

They are described in the following sutras.

7. The three ways of acquiring valid knowledge are direct perception, inference as the result of observation, and learning from others who are knowledgeable.

Direct perception results in immediate knowing of what is observed. When circumstances or concepts are analyzed and we use our powers of reasoning to determine what is true, what is thought to be true should be carefully examined and verified. Learning from others who are knowledgeable is a convenient way of acquiring reliable knowledge. For a person who is intent on the spiritual path, a knowledgeable guru can be helpful. If such a teacher is not readily available, useful knowledge can be acquired by direct perception as a result of intellectual inquiry, intuitive insight, or personal experience.

8. Illusions are inaccurate perceptions.

Inaccurate or incomplete perception of what is observed results in illusions which may be retained in the mind as false information that interferes with rational thinking.

The primary obstacle to Self-realization is a flawed sense of Self-identity. When this error is corrected, a truth seeker's awareness is immediately restored to wholeness. The ultimate aim of right spiritual practice is to see through, and transcend, the illusional sense of Self.

9. Delusions are erroneous mental concepts. Hallucinations and fantasies are entirely subjective perceptions not based on anything that exists.

Erroneous ideas and beliefs cloud and distort awareness, interfere with rational thinking, obstruct endeavors to know what is true, and may compel unwise or erratic behaviors.

Hallucinations are mind- or brain-produced phenomena which may manifest as mental or audible voices that seem to be real, visions, or other distortions of perception.

Fantasies may occur when attention and imagination are not controlled.

A truth seeker should avoid delusions, hallucinations, and fantasies by cultivating psychological health, being willing to confront and discern what is true, adhering to a regimen of meaningful activity balanced by interludes of rest and wholesome recreation, and nurturing spiritual awareness.

10. Sleep is a modification of the power of cognition.

Powers of cognition (perception that provides knowledge) are usually restricted when we sleep to allow the body to be refreshed and the mind to organize information that has been newly acquired. As we become more spiritually aware, we can sleep superconsciously instead of being identified with subconscious or unconscious states.

11. Memories are mental impressions of prior perceptions.

All perceptions leave impressions in the mind that can be elicited (brought forth into conscious awareness) and may be influential even when we are not consciously aware of them. Influential memories that are accumulated over a period of time comprise a karmic (potentially causative) condition. If allowed to be influential, their effects may be constructive and life-enhancing or restrictive and troublesome. If their effects are constructive and life-enhancing in accord with our major purposes, they can be allowed to be influential. How to definitely eliminate the causes of troublesome subconscious influences is described in the following sutra.

12. The troublesome influences of mental impressions should be restrained, weakened, and removed by meditation practice and dispassionate nonattachment.

Both disciplines should be appropriately used.

13. Alert concentration on a chosen object is meditation.

Because of our innate inclination to be attentive to what is perceived, the easiest way to avoid being unduly influenced by troublesome mental modifications is to concentrate on what is of greater value. To meditatively contemplate the pure-conscious essence of our being and the reality of God is of greatest value.

14. Meditation becomes stable by devoted, persistent practice.

Beginning meditators are usually advised to sit for twenty to thirty minutes to allow enough time for the body to relax, the mind to become calm, attention to be concentrated, and a clear state of mind and consciousness to prevail. Devotional ardor and strong resolve that empowers and motivates soon enables a meditator to be firmly established in practice.

15. Dispassionate nonattachment enables one to consciously control urges, cravings, and instinctual drives.

Self-mastery is essential for one who aspires to Self- and God-realization. Objective, rational, unemotional observation of our thoughts, feelings, and inclinations enables us to view them with detachment, make right choices, effectively live as we desire to live, and skillfully meditate.

In the course of everyday living, and when meditating, it is helpful to disregard what is not essential or important. When meditating, dispassionate disregard of thoughts, feelings, and subjective perceptions is recommended.

16. Higher [and more easily practiced] detachment results from Self-realization that makes one impervious to the influences of cosmic forces.

Transformations and changes that occur in the mind and awareness can also be caused by subtle influences of cosmic forces regulated by three primary attributes of the Oversoul which extend throughout the cosmos.

The Sanskrit names for the three attributes are *sattwa*, *rajas*, and *tamas*. Sattwic influences purify the mind, clarify awareness, and enhance intellectual and intuitive powers. Rajasic influences stimulate and energize the mind, emotions, and body. Tamasic influences cloud awareness, dull the mind, blur intellectual and intuitive powers, and cause thoughts and feelings of apathetic disinterest to arise.

When sattwic influences prevail during meditation, we are inclined to be inspired and alert, concentration is more easily focused, and superconscious states may be experienced. When we are not meditating, sattwic influences incline us to adhere to a wholesome lifestyle and be optimistic and cheerful.

Rajasic influences arouse emotions, make the mind restless, and cause attention to be easily distracted. Tamasic influences may cause feelings of heaviness and a tendency to be passive or semiconscious. These influences can be resisted and restrained by concentrating with inspired intention and fervent devotion until a superconscious state is experienced.

17. As fluctuations in awareness cease to be influential, one may experience samadhi along with subtle thoughts, partial Self-knowledge, and perceptions of bliss.

This a preliminary stage during which various perceptions are present, including random thoughts and feelings which may be subtle. Although this samadhi may be accompanied by enjoyable perceptions, it has modifying characteristics and influences of cosmic forces regulated by the gunas. Although it can provide useful insights and perceptions of possibilities yet to be realized, it does not liberate our consciousness. It should not to be considered as the ultimate attainment nor be allowed to cause attachments to feelings or subtle perceptions.

The four preliminary stages of samadhi that may be experienced are:

1. *Comparative*. With thoughts, ideas, memories, and feelings that provide pleasure or enjoyment. One may be inclined to compare their perceptions with prior meditative perceptions or with what others have said about superconscious states.
2. *Noncomparitive*. Without memories or ideas that interfere with contemplative concentration. Attention and awareness are so fully absorbed in the object of contemplation that all sense of difference or otherness is absent.
3. *Reflective*. Examination of subtle essences or attributes of what is contemplated, with feelings or emotions present. One may inquire into subtle aspects of the mind, intellect, ego, processes of cosmic manifestation, or higher realties. The sense that "I am observing this" remains.
4. *Spontaneously revealed knowledge*. The subtle essences and aspects of consciousness are directly comprehended. What was formerly only observed is flawlessly reflected in the meditator's awareness.

Beyond these stages is pure realization of oneness without the support of an object of perception. When this realization is flawless and permanent, it persists after meditation practice during normal activities. Constant Self- and God-realization culminates in liberation of consciousness.

18. The other [higher] samadhi leaves constructive impressions in the mind.

The influences of constructive superconscious impressions resist, weaken, neutralize, and dissolve all of the troublesome subconscious conditionings that were impressed into the mind by ordinary experiences.

19. From samadhi without complete knowledge one may progress to more refined states of samadhi or again become involved with gross characteristics of nature and its actions.

When Self-realization is not flawless, even if thoughts and other objects of perception are not observed, a meditator may still be inclined to be preoccupied with investigating subtle characteristics of nature. From this level, one may transcend all objects of perception or again become involved with them.

20. Higher samadhi is preceded by disciplined endeavor, attentive meditation practice, insights, unobstructed memory [of prior subtle perceptions], unwavering faith, and the unveiling and emergence of innate knowledge.

Disciplined, concentrated endeavor on the spiritual path is essential and meditation practice must be attentive. Insights provide useful knowledge. Vivid memories of prior insightful perceptions support our ongoing endeavors. Faith that does not waver eliminates the possibility of doubt and indecision about spiritual practice. Innate knowledge is unveiled and emerges because of right practice, superconscious influences, and spontaneous soul awakenings that occur.

21. For one whose progress is fast and whose practice is intensive, samadhi is near.

Spiritual practice is intensive when aspiration to be fully Self-realized is supported by endeavors that produce desired results. Self-realization should not be thought of as a possible distant-future goal to be attained; it should be considered as a natural state to which to quickly awaken.

22. Progress is in accord with intensity of practice, whether mild, medium, or extremely intensive.

Practice is extremely intensive when nonessential matters are disregarded and attention and actions are concentrated on the purposes to be accomplished.

23. Samadhi is quickly realized by devotional surrender to God.

Surrender of the mistaken sense of Self is the direct way to having awareness restored to wholeness. If God is thought of as being other than what we are, we may experience a sense of communion with that concept of God. If God is acknowledged as the omnipresent Reality in which we abide as an individualized unit, surrender to it will result in realization of oneness. Surrender of the illusional sense of Self occurs more easily by aspiring to be conscious of being *in* God rather than to be unified *with* God. Thinking that God is separate from us is an obstacle to God-realization.

24. God [the Cosmic Soul] is not influenced or restricted by karma.

Because God's cosmic forces produced and regulate the universe, the reality of God is not influenced by the effects of causes that it originates. The transcendent reality of God is pure existence beyond space-time. God's expressive aspects allow specialized actions to occur.

Seven aspects of God are *subjective*, one is *objective*. It is helpful to know about them before they are intellectually or intuitively discerned. You will then be able to know what is being perceived as insights emerge in your awareness.

The first two *subjective* aspects produce and pervade the causal realm of electric and magnetic forces.

The third and fourth *subjective* aspects produce and pervade the astral realm of energies and life forces.

The fifth and sixth *subjective* aspects express as the subtle attributes which have potential to produce the gross material attributes of a physical universe.

The seventh *subjective* aspect is the presence of God that pervades everything that is manifested. Although it cannot be seen, we can be aware of it and know that we abide in it.

The eighth, and *objective* aspect, is Cosmic Individuality which emanates cosmic forces that produce the material components of a universe. The reality of God extends from the field of absolute existence-being to the physical realm.

25. God's omniscience is unsurpassed.

God, all-knowing, all-powerful, and all-pervading, cannot be compared to any relative phenomena.

26. Transcending time, God is the guru of the ancient teachers.

Full knowledge of God and of cosmic processes is innate to every soul. It is unveiled, and can be actualized, by right living and right spiritual practice. Thus, it is said that God is the true guru. Philosophical concepts, lifestyle regimens, and spiritual practices can be learned from others; liberating knowledge is Self-revealed.

27. The evidential indication of God is Om.

The vibration of the power of supreme Consciousness is evidence of that which emanates it.

The Sanskrit word Om has four "measures" or parts (*a, u, m,* and the dot above the letter *m* which signifies a nasal sound when chanted). These four parts are related to four states of consciousness: waking, dreaming, sleeping, and the state of pure Self-knowing.

28. One should vocally and mentally chant Om, attentively listen to it, meditatively contemplate it, comprehend its real nature, and identify with it.

Vocal and mental chanting of Om, with attention focused in the front and higher brain calms the mind and improves concentration.

When attention is internalized and vocal chanting ceases, subtle sound-frequencies may be heard in the ears (or around the head). Meditation on Om can then proceed by endeavoring to hear a subtle sound-frequency behind the first sound that is heard, then a subtle sound behind each sound that emerges. When a constant sound is heard, it can be used as a self-manifesting mantra in which to merge attention and awareness while contemplating that which is beyond it: pure consciousness.

29. By meditation on God, all obstacles are removed and the reality of God is realized.

Meditation to the stage of God-communion removes attention and awareness from modified mental states and weakens and dissolves subconscious conditions that distort awareness.

Meditation on God can begin with contemplation of God as God is felt, thought, or imagined to be. As we become more insightful, concepts of God are replaced by direct knowledge of God as God is.

30. Some obstacles to experiencing samadhi are doubt, negligence, confusion, failure to make progress, instability, addictions and attachments, misperceptions, and distractions of attention.

Many obstacles to spiritual growth can be removed by our right endeavors.

To avoid or heal physical illness, lifestyle regimens which contribute to health and vitality should be chosen.

Doubt can be replaced with faith.

The habit of negligence can be corrected by adopting constructive mental attitudes and personal behaviors.

Philosophical confusion can be eliminated by acquiring accurate information about God, our true Self-identity, cosmic processes, and how to nurture divine qualities.

Spiritual awakening can be quickened by right living and right meditation practice.

Mental and emotional instability can be replaced with peace of mind, self-confidence, and emotional maturity.

Addictions can be renounced by resolute choice and by nurturing spiritual growth.

31. Symptoms of distracted attention are anxiety, frustration, restless movements of the body, and irregular breathing.

When we are not Self-knowing, we are inclined to identify with something. If our purposes and intentions are not clearly defined, our attention is inclined to aimlessly wander. When first sitting to meditate, remember the purpose of practice and focus your attention on it with firm resolve.

32. To overcome these obstacles one can meditatively concentrate on a chosen object or ideal.

When concentration on a meditative object is focused, the mind is calmed, emotions are easily regulated, deep physical relaxation prevails, stress is reduced, breathing becomes smooth and refined, and subliminal influences that formerly stimulated the nervous system and mind become dormant.

At other times, distractions can be avoided by choosing to be cheerful, optimistic, alert and attentive, and to live with a clear sense of purposes which are of superior value.

33. The mind is purified by cultivating thoughts and feelings of friendship for others, compassion for those who are suffering, happiness for the well-being that others enjoy, and dispassion regarding what is observed.

Cultivating these virtuous qualities provides peace of mind and emotional stability. Cultivate the habit of acknowledging the innate divine nature of everyone you know or think about and be friendly and supportive in personal relationships.

Have compassion for others who experience misfortune and pray for their highest good to be actualized.

Be happy and thankful for the well-being and fortunate circumstances that others have.

Objectively view events and circumstances without being emotionally disturbed or distracted from your aims in life or your duties to others. When events or circumstances require your response, act skillfully and appropriately while going forward to accomplish your purposes.

34. Or one may definitely overcome all such obstacles by practice of pranayama.

Pranayama can be practiced by regulating inhalation and exhalation to encourage the body's life-forces to flow freely. The mind is then calmed, emotions are settled, the body is relaxed, and awareness can be alert and attentive.

The following pranayama may be practiced when starting to meditate, or anytime when its beneficial effects are desired.

Sit upright. Inhale deeply and exhale. With the thumb of the right hand, close the right nostril and smoothly inhale through the left nostril. Pause a moment. With a finger, close the left nostril and smoothly exhale through the right nostril. Pause for a moment. Inhale through the right nostril. Pause. Exhale through the left nostril. Repeat this routine eight or ten times. To conclude, inhale deeply through both nostrils. Exhale, and relax.

This practice encourages an even flow of air through both nostrils and harmonious interactions to occur between the two hemispheres of the brain.

When we are in good health, for approximately two hours air flows through one nostril more freely. Air then flows more freely through the other nostril for approximately two hours. This is because, from time to time, the erectile tissue in one nostril swells slightly and partially blocks the flow of air.

When air flows more freely through the right nostril, the body is somewhat heated; the left hemisphere of the brain is more dominant; thinking is more orderly and rational; and attention and actions are inclined to be outwardly directed.

When air flows more freely through the left nostril, the body is somewhat cooled; the right hemisphere of the brain is more dominant; attention is inclined to be inward, subjective, and reflective; thinking is usually more imaginative and intuitive.

When air flows evenly through both nostrils, interactions between both hemispheres of the brain tend to be balanced; mental alertness and emotional calmness are more likely to be experienced; concentration is easier.

Initiated truth seekers in the kriya yoga tradition which I represent are taught a pranayama which enables them to circulate life force through the central channel in the spinal pathway and into the higher brain. Diligent practice of this unique meditation technique calms the mind, internalizes attention, improves powers of concentration, and refines the nervous system.

35. Subtle subjective perceptions contribute to mental stability.

Subtle intellectual and intuitive perceptions and insights that improve our understanding of our true nature and our relationship to God and the universe clarify our awareness, calm the mind, and enable us to think more rationally.

36. Changes that contribute to mental stability also naturally occur because of the luminosity of mind and awareness that prevails.

Superconscious influences cause beneficial psychological changes to spontaneously occur. Before and after proficiency in superconscious meditation practice is acquired, mental and emotional well-being should be nurtured.

37. Mental stability can also be experienced by contemplating the states of consciousness and virtuous attitudes and behaviors of spiritually enlightened saints and sages.

Inquire: What is it like to be Self-realized? What will I think and feel? What will I do? How will I be when I am spiritually enlightened?"

What is your intuitive response? Can you imagine what it is like to be Self- and God-realized? Ponder the possibilities. Expand your mind and awareness. Mentally "see" yourself as being spiritually awake. Imagine how you will feel, how you will live, and what you might do when you are spiritually enlightened without limitations. Believe that you can be like that.

38. Also, by acquiring knowledge of sleep and dream states.

By examining states of consciousness, useful knowledge of them can be acquired. When our consciousness is ordinary, we are usually only aware when we are awake, dimly aware of our dreams, unaware of what occurs during interludes of deep sleep, and not familiar with superconscious states.

As skill in experiencing superconscious states is acquired and intellectual and intuitive powers are improved, the full range of consciousness will be comprehended.

39. The mind is stabilized and awareness is clarified by steady meditation on one, chosen object of attention.

The contents of the mind become orderly and awareness becomes clear when attention is completely involved with one object of interest. If what is thought about or contemplated is not attractive, or does not arouse curiosity and inspire a strong resolve to discover the truth about it or identify with it, attention will not flow easily to it.

40. Proficient practice of samadhi enables one to acquire mastery of attention and to perceive that which is small and that which is of ultimate magnitude.

When powers of concentration are developed, accurate knowledge of what is observed can be perceived. As the mind is purified and consciousness expands and becomes cosmic conscious, knowledge of categories and processes of cosmic manifestation and higher realities can be acquired.

41. Clarified awareness accurately reflects what is perceived.

Awareness is related to a thought, mental concept, feeling, or thing which attracts our attention. When our awareness is pure, it accurately reflects its object and presents it to our mind and consciousness. When awareness is blurred, its reflections are distorted. Inaccurate information is then received by the mind and illusions are mistaken for facts.

42. When mental transformations persist and awareness is not tranquil, insights, perceptions, random thoughts, and illusions can be intermingled.

When modifying fluctuations in the mind and awareness exist, the conditions described in this sutra may prevail along with superconscious perceptions. When the mind is calm and attention is concentrated, they will be less forceful.

43. When samadhi without mental transformations is steady, the awareness of the meditator reflects [only] the reality of pure consciousness.

In the early stages of samadhi, the mind is illumined by the light (reality) of one's pure-conscious essence of being. When higher samadhi is stable, instead of perceiving the reflected image of one's true Self, flawless Self-knowing prevails. There is then no awareness of being other than pure consciousness.

44. Thus, both kinds of samadhi are explained.

The first kind of samadhi is impure because it is modified by mental transformations and concepts, emotions, or subtle subjective perceptions. The second kind is pure or absolute.

Many meditators make the mistake of being satisfied with the experiences provided by the first kind of samadhi because they enjoy visions and pleasurable sensations or what seems to them to be communion with higher realities.

45. The possibility of samadhi being mixed with subtle perceptions exists until external influences are transcended.

Even when mental and emotional influences are absent, the mind and awareness can be disturbed by the actions of cosmic forces (as explained in sutra 16 of this chapter).

46. These samadhi states are supported by objects of perception.

Because of having a history of being aware of, and relating to, objective circumstances, it may be difficult to imagine what it is like to be conscious without being identified with something. Until Self-realization is complete and permanent, it can be helpful to ask: Is there anything beyond what I have thus far realized that I should know and experience? And be receptive to what can unfold.

47. When awareness is purified, the reality of the Self is revealed.

When obstacles to the actualization of our pure-conscious essence are absent, Self-realization spontaneously blossoms.

48. One then has flawless knowledge of what is true.

Accurate knowledge of our true nature and the reality of God emerges from within us.

49. Knowledge acquired by ordinary modes of learning is different from knowledge that results from samadhi.

Knowledge acquired by observation, reasoning, reflection, experimentation, and from others, may be flawed or misinterpreted. Innate knowledge of higher realities that emerges into our purified awareness is flawless.

50. Mental impressions produced by samadhi inhibit, weaken, and dissolve harmful mental impressions and produce permanent, beneficial changes.

Even when thinking is rational, metaphysical concepts are understood, and everyday life is enjoyable, one who is intent on liberation of consciousness should regularly meditate until superconscious influences completely purify the mind.

51. When gross mental impressions are dissolved, constructive mental impressions of samadhi also dissolve. Samadhi without the support of an object of perception is then steady.

This pure samadhi, the highest degree of accomplishment that can result from attentive meditation practice, is not the final stage of spiritual awakening. The ultimate (last, furthest extent) stage is realized when the clarity of consciousness that prevails during meditative samadhi can be maintained at all times when one is not meditating.

CHAPTER TWO

Kriya Yoga

Intensive Spiritual Practice

1. Intensive self-discipline, studious Self-inquiry, and surrender to God are the practices of kriya yoga.

   Mastery of attention, mental states, emotions, sense urges, and behaviors frees mind and awareness from conditions which confine and restrict it.

   Insightful study of higher realities provides knowledge of our true nature, the reality of God, and cosmic processes. To live effectively, knowledge of the laws of cause and effect that determine events and circumstances in the mundane realm should also be acquired.

   Surrender of the illusional sense of Self-identity to God is accomplished by nurturing devotion to the ideal of being Self- and God-realized that culminates in transcendence of ego-consciousness. Attention and awareness are then unified with supreme Consciousness.

   Kriyas are intentional actions that nurture personal well-being, emotional maturity, and spiritual growth.

   I am frequently contacted by individuals who express their interest in learning kriya yoga practices. They usually want to learn meditation techniques; they seldom know that complete practice of kriya yoga includes all of the practices described in this chapter. Practice of meditation without the support of all of the recommended practices is not complete and cannot produce soul-satisfying results.

A truth seeker who desires to practice kriya yoga should be:

- Sincere: honest and unpretentious (not inclined to dramatize attitudes or behaviors to attract attention to themselves or to impress others with overt acts of religious devotion).
- Respectful of the kriya yoga tradition and the teachers who represent it.
- Devoid of egotism (an inflated sense of self-importance) and mental perversity (an inclination to distort what is learned to serve egocentric interests).
- Receptive to learning.
- Sufficiently intelligent to comprehend what is taught.
- Willing to practice what is learned.
- Have the capacity to skillfully practice what is learned.

2. Kriya yoga is practiced to weaken and eliminate all obstacles to Self- and God-realization.

Our constructive actions do not cause our spiritual growth; they provide ideal conditions that allow it to naturally occur. When the mind is purified and awareness has been clarified by diligent kriya yoga practices, rapid spiritual growth occurs because the innate urge to be Self- and God-realized can then be influential. Forceful effort should not be used. All that is required is sustained aspiration to be Self-realized and faithful adherence to the recommended practices.

3. Some restrictions which can cause suffering and interfere with endeavors to be Self- and God-realized are egoism, illusions, attachments, aversions, and confusion about birth and death.

The primary cause of human suffering and misfortune is inaccurate or incomplete perception of our essence of being and our relationship with God and the universe. When the body is healthy, there may be psychological suffering. Fear of change, misfortune, or death can cause mental and emotional distress. Even when all material circumstances are ideal, their eventual ending is certain because nothing in the mundane realm is permanent. Confronting the facts of life should not cause us to be pessimistic or fearful; we should be highly motivated to improve our understanding and learn how to wisely relate to them.

4. Inability to accurately perceive what is true is the primary cause of other restrictions, which may be dormant, weak, controlled, or freely influential.

Subliminal conditions that prevent spiritual growth result from flawed perception and incomplete understanding. Those which are dormant may be activated and cause problems in the future or may be eradicated when understanding is improved. Those which are weak may easily be overcome. Those which are controlled can be more easily weakened or eliminated. Those which are strongly influential can also be weakened and removed by using our powers of discriminative intelligence and by super-conscious meditation practice that results in the emergence of Self-knowledge.

5. Lack of knowledge of what is true causes one to erroneously presume that which is noneternal to be eternal, that which is impure to be pure, that which is painful to be pleasurable, and the ego to be the real Self.

The erroneous ideas described in this sutra are common to many people whose awareness is ordinary.

6. Egoism results from undiscerning identification with mind and matter.

Egocentric states of consciousness prevail when thinking and behaviors are allowed to be determined by narrow self-interests. *Egocentricity* is caused by an illusional (mistaken) sense of Self acquired when a unit of pure consciousness was individualized and its awareness was blurred because of over-identification with the attributes of the field of primordial nature. *Egotism* is an inflated sense of self-importance.

Egotism is easier to discard than egocentricity: it diminishes when emotional maturity is actualized. An egocentric sense of Self-identity confines awareness and is often reinforced by associating with others whose Self-sense is similarly flawed.

Because an illusional sense of Self is the primary cause of lack of spiritual awareness, the fundamental purpose of yoga (samadhi) practice is to allow the truth seeker to see through or rise above it.

7. Preoccupation with pleasurable sensations produces affection for them that causes attachments.

When we are strongly attached to pleasurable behaviors or relationships we may forget that all mundane conditions are temporary; that their absence may cause us to experience discomfort or pain. Dedicated spiritual aspirants are advised to express creatively and relate to others appropriately without becoming addicted to what is done or experienced. Purposeful activities and meaningful relationships can be life-enhancing and enjoyable when we are Self-aware rather than egocentric or emotionally dependent.

8. Aversion is dislike of, and a desire to avoid, that which caused or may cause discomfort or pain.

It is natural to want to avoid circumstances that threaten our well-being or survival. It is not spiritually beneficial to allow erratic emotional reactions to disturb our soul peace or elicit behaviors which complicate our lives or the lives of others.

Aversion-responses should be appropriate to the situation rather than allowed to be impulsively compelled by thoughts or feelings of likes and dislikes or prejudiced opinions.

9. An inherent will to live is compelling even when it is known that physical death will eventually occur.

The innate inclination of all beings is to thrive, flourish, and be continuously happy. While at the core of our being we know we are immortal, we are also conscious of the fact that the duration of physical life is limited. If we could live in this material world for hundreds, thousands, or millions of years, we would eventually have to leave it when the forces of the universe are withdrawn into the primordial field of nature.

The best way to prepare for eventual transition from the body, and for whatever else we are destined to experience in the near or distant future, is to nurture spiritual awareness until we are fully Self- and God-conscious.

The best way to consciously withdraw from the body when we must do so, is to calmly withdraw attention and awareness from external conditions, bring our life forces up through the spinal pathway, have attention and awareness established in the crown chakra (higher brain), listen to the Om vibration, and melt into the transcendental field of pure Consciousness.

10. Subtle restricting influences can be overcome by restoring them to their origins.

Restricting influences that are barely discernible because of their weakness can be easily subdued and made harmless by gentle use of will power, intentional performance of right actions, and attentive practice of superconscious meditation.

11. Gross restricting influences can be resisted and eliminated by self-analysis, practice of samadhi, and awakened knowledge.

The causes of restricting influences can be discovered and the influences restored to an inactive state by a gentle act of intention; being Self-aware rather than egocentric; cultivating mental and emotional calmness; avoiding illusions; improving intellectual and intuitive powers; renouncing harmful habits and strong or sentimental attachments; and acting wisely.

Subliminal, causative, restricting influences are like seeds that have potential to flourish. Seeds of plants in nature are nourished by nutrients and water. Mental seeds (impressions) with potential to be restrictive that were planted in the soil of the subconscious mind by perceptions and experiences are nourished by emotions and thoughts, and by our actions and reactions similar to those which first impressed them in the mind. Their powers can be diminished and neutralized by cultivating mental states, thoughts, feelings, and actions that are constructive.

Troublesome influences are effortlessly resisted and their forces weakened and dissolved by superconscious influences that prevail when, and after, samadhi states are experienced.

Gradual or sudden emergence of our innate knowledge of what is true replaces erroneous ideas and illusions.

12. Accumulated mental impressions [karmic patterns] rooted in the primary restriction may cause effects in this and other life-cycles.

The words *karma* and *kriya* are derived from the Sanskrit verb root "to do" (to cause and effect). The primary influence that restricts awareness is the mistaken sense of Self. Karmic mental impressions may influence thoughts, emotional states, actions, and reactions when awareness is ordinary or blurred. They cannot influence us when we are constantly Self-aware and our thoughts and actions are Self-determined.

13. For as long as they [restrictive mental impressions] exist, they may cause either pain or pleasure.

14. Pleasure or pain, joy or sorrow, may result from the effects of karmic influences according to their character and quality.

When subliminal influences are allowed to be expressive, our experiences tend to be conformed to their characteristics and the intensity of their strength. Their effects may provide pleasure, cause distress, or be of minor significance.

15. Because of the existence of latent mental impressions and the influences of cosmic forces, the possibility of pain exists even in the midst of pleasurable circumstances.

Until dormant, troublesome subliminal conditionings are dissolved, they may be activated and cause discomfort in the near or distant future. They may be activated by memories, ideas, feelings, or circumstances similar to those which first impressed them in the mind, or when we are tired, confused, emotionally unstable, angry, frustrated, our energy levels are low, we have been deprived of sleep or food, or are ill.

16. Suffering which has not yet been experienced is to be avoided.

Painful events can be avoided by 1) removing their causes; 2) rising above their causes; 3) causing or allowing events that are more desirable to occur.

Obvious causes of misfortune may be easily banished. A negative mental attitude can be replaced with optimism and expectations of good fortune. Unproductive actions can be replaced with actions that produce desired results. Laziness can be replaced with energetic enthusiasm. Physical health can be improved by adhering to health-promoting regimens. Poverty can be avoided by cultivating prosperity attitudes and behaviors. Loneliness or despair can be avoided by cultivating Self-reliance and wholesome relationships. Feelings of grief can be replaced with higher understanding.

Rational thinking, constructive living, and superconscious meditation practice weakens harmful karmic influences and replaces them with beneficial influences. As Self-realization becomes pronounced and permanent, karmic conditions become less influential. We can then live freely, choose our actions and circumstances, and increasingly be conscious of having the support of the life-enhancing impulses of supreme Consciousness commonly referred to as God's grace.

At this stage of spiritual awakening, karmic patterns that may still exist in the mind are mostly dormant. They can be dispassionately confronted and released if they are activated or they will be dissolved by superconscious influences.

17. The primary cause of suffering is mistaken Self-identity.

Intellectual comprehension of our true nature is helpful. Intuitive perception of our true nature is more helpful. Self-realization is of ultimate value.

Intellectual comprehension and intuitive perception of the truth of what we are enables us to more skillfully relate to, and solve, problems and difficulties that result from a sense of ego identification that has not yet been overcome. When innate knowledge of our true nature prevails, the primary cause of suffering disappears.

18. The three constituent attributes innate to the elements of nature and expressive in the sense organs have the characteristics of luminosity, transformative action, and inertia.

Note: For more information about the characteristics of the three constituent attributes of nature, see chapter one, sutra 16. Also, *guna* in the glossary.

19. The phases of the primary cosmic forces are specialized; not specialized; that which is only indicated; and unmanifested.

The sixteen specialized aspects are the gross expressions of earth, water, fire, air (gases), and space with cosmic forces; five capacities of the senses (of smelling, touching, hearing, seeing, and tasting); five capacities of action (of movement in space, grasping, speech, reproduction, and elimination); and a mind, which is a particularized unit of Cosmic or Universal Mind.

The six unspecialized aspects are the five subtle states of the specialized aspects (described in the preceding paragraph) which precede their gross manifestation, and ego or illusional sense of Self-identity.

The indicated aspect, known by its presence, is the faculty which makes possible intellectual determination and enables the mind-identified soul to acquire knowledge.

The fine aspects of cosmic forces devoid of characteristics

remain in the field of primordial nature (the Om vibration and its self-originated attributes) and make possible the periodic emanations of a universe.

20. The seer, while observing what is seen, remains pure.

As individualized units of pure consciousness, our essence of being never changes. As God is not influenced by natural phenomena, so our essence of being is not influenced by what we observe. Only our awareness (which reflects perceptions) and our mind can be influenced by perceptions.

21. A universe exists to provide souls a field in which to express.

A universe that is emanated from supreme Consciousness through the medium of primordial nature (the Om vibration and its self-manifested attributes of space, time, and fine cosmic forces) exists as a field in which God's consciousness and aspects are expressive. A universe can exist for billions or trillions of years until the cosmos is withdrawn into the field of primordial nature and its attributes are restored to a state of equilibrium until another universe is emanated. Souls which were not spiritually enlightened prior to the dissolution of a universe may again become involved with a new universe where their mundane experiences and spiritual growth can continue. There is a pure realm beyond the field of primordial nature where almost-enlightened souls which are not completely awakened to the stage of absolute realization can reside.

22. The universe is not perceived by those who have transcended it; it continues to be perceived by all who abide in it.

We relate to the physical realm while we are here; we do not see it after we have departed. While it is possible for some souls in astral realms to mentally and spiritually communicate with souls in the physical world, this does not commonly occur.

23. Interactions between the pure essence of supreme Consciousness and the forces of nature cause units of pure consciousness to be individualized.

The enlivening aspect of supreme Consciousness that shines on and is reflected from the field of primordial nature continuously produces units of pure consciousness. Units of pure consciousness which are identified with objective nature inhabit causal, astral, and physical realms and flow between them as they experience events of entry and departure which are commonly referred to as birth and death.

24. Lack of Self-awareness causes a mistaken sense of Self.

Units of pure consciousness identified with cosmic forces and aspects of nature that have assumed an illusional sense of independent selfhood are referred to as souls. It is only the deluded soul nature that is in need of being "saved" from a condition of limitation; our essence of being is ever pure.

For many centuries, philosophers and theologians have promoted a variety of theories regarding the means by which confused souls might be able to have a conscious relationship with God. Believing a religious creed or doctrine cannot solve the problem, nor can mechanical performance of ritual, good works, blind faith, unenlightened prayer, passive meditation practice, or devotion to someone who is presumed to be a savior. The only way to have awareness restored to wholeness is to awaken through the stages of spiritual growth: from ordinary awareness to Self-realization, God-realization, and liberation of consciousness.

25. Removal of the illusional sense of Self results in liberation of consciousness.

Liberation of consciousness occurs when Self-awareness is no longer identified with ego-consciousness, modified mental states, the constituent attributes of nature, and cosmic forces.

26. Unwavering intuitive knowledge of the reality of God removes all delusions and illusions.

Partial insights of higher realities and interludes of God-communion are beneficial: constant knowledge of the reality of God is redemptive and liberating.

27. Liberating intuitive insights may occur in seven stages.

At the first stage, we discern the restrictive conditions that must be removed and are inclined to commit to concentrated, constructive spiritual practice.

At the second stage, restrictions which have the potential to cause suffering or misfortune are weakened to the extent that they are no longer influential.

At the third stage, superconscious states which enable us to examine the fine characteristics of our consciousness are frequently experienced.

At the fourth stage, when meditating we can comprehend our relationship to the mind and to internal and external phenomena, and experience episodes of Self-realization.

At the fifth stage, mental impressions no longer modify or cause changes in awareness. Self-realization is constant and episodes of cosmic consciousness may be experienced.

The sixth stage is God-realization. Cosmic forces regulated by the three constituent attributes of nature no longer cause changes in our awareness.

The seventh stage is complete liberation of consciousness.

28. Practice of yoga eliminates obstacles to Self-knowledge.

Samadhi is the highest yoga practice. The disciplines that precede, and make one's mind and consciousness receptive to samadhi, are described in the following sutras.

29. Refraining from harmful behaviors, faithful adherence to constructive practices, firm meditation posture, pranayama practice, internalized attention, concentration, meditation, and samadhi are the eight limbs of yoga practice.

These eight aspects of practice comprise the path of Raja Yoga (a superior way to elicit spiritual growth) that results in spiritual enlightenment. When they are fully actualized, we more easily experience total well-being, orderly relationships with others and our environment, the support of nature, and rapid spiritual awakening.

30. Harmlessness; truthfulness; non-stealing; conscious control and right use of vital forces; and nonattachment are the five restraints to cultivate and actualize.

These attitudes and behaviors are normal for a person who is healthy-minded and spiritually conscious. If they are not yet actualized by a truth seeker, they should definitely be attentively cultivated.

31. Their application is not limited by time or cultural conditions.

The necessity for the cultivation and actualization of these attitudes and behaviors is not limited to the era in which we live or by cultural conditions because they represent the ideal, responsible way for everyone to live.

32. Purity; contentment; self-discipline; Self-inquiry; and surrender to God are the five intentional practices to maintain.

Cultivation of these intentional practices makes mastery of the five restraints easier; cultivation of the five restraints supports our resolve to maintain the intentional practices.

33. To weaken and neutralize harmful inclinations, replace them with constructive actions.

The easiest way to control and overcome the influences of harmful subconscious inclinations is to nurture feelings of happiness and self-confidence and to intentionally perform constructive actions.

An optimistic mental attitude enables us to be receptive to experiencing ideal outcomes for all situations. Happiness and self-confidence clarify awareness, improve mental abilities and powers of perception, enable functional skills to be used more effectively, and strengthen the body's immune system.

Cultivation of the five restraints and the five intentional practices are the constructive actions that support all other spiritual practices.

34. The forcefulness of instinctual and subliminal inclinations, and of mental conflicts and memories of physical, mental, or emotional pain related to one's past actions or the actions of others may be mild, moderate, or strong, and may cause pain or suffering, They can be overcome by choosing and performing opposing actions.

Memories, thoughts, and emotions that cause pain should be replaced with thoughts and feelings that are constructive, enjoyable, and life-enhancing. Psychic (soul) forces that are confined in the mind with memories of pain, failure, rejection, or other unpleasant experiences, are then released.

If painful memories are due to mistreatment or abuse by others, forgive them, and release them to their highest good. If painful memories are due to your mistakes or inappropriate behaviors, forgive yourself and go forward with confidence.

Whatever has to be confronted that is in the storehouse of your mind, confront and resolve it. The more knowledgeable and spiritually aware you are, the easier it will be to relate to, and rise above, the influences of past events and the urges and desires that arise in your awareness which you know to be incompatible with your aspirations and purposes.

35. In the presence of one whose thoughts and actions are harmless, all living things become peaceful and harmless.

When we are firmly established in harmlessness (*ahimsa*), our thoughts, feelings, and actions are entirely constructive. The peacefulness that we radiate into the mental atmosphere calms the minds and emotions of people and all forms of sentient life.

36. One who is truthful experiences quick results of actions.

Conforming our thoughts and actions to what we know to be true keeps our attention and our actions focused on useful goals and productive endeavors that are easily actualized. If we are not yet truth-conscious, mental confusion, emotional conflict, and erratic behaviors may result.

In personal relationships, truthful individuals are reliable; untruthful individuals are not trustworthy.

37. One who does not steal, and has no thoughts of stealing from others, experiences prosperity and good fortune.

Stealing, taking something from someone to whom it rightfully belongs, causes hardship for the victim and inclines a dishonest person to have thoughts and feelings of guilt and remorse.

Honest, emotionally mature individuals who choose to be responsible for their actions and are optimistically receptive to good fortune can easily prosper in all aspects of their lives.

Harmonious integration of the spiritual, mental, physical, emotional, and environmental aspects of life enables us to be in the flow of necessary resources and supportive events and circumstances that are for our highest good.

38. When all thoughts and actions are fully conformed to one's aspiration to be Self-realized, physical, mental, and spiritual strength is acquired.

Brahmacharya, the Sanskrit word used in the original text, is "Godly conduct" that is recommended for one who aspires to Self-realization. When mental powers and vital forces are conserved rather than wasted, gross energies are transmuted into fine essences that strengthen the body's immune system, refine the brain, enliven the nervous system, slow biologic aging processes, and greatly improve powers of perception, intelligence, will, and concentration.

Worry, stress, purposeless actions, compulsive behaviors,

mental confusion, emotional conflicts, overeating, excessive fasting, addictive behaviors, excessive talking, lack of sleep, poor health habits, and toxic environmental conditions drain vital forces from the body.

39. As attachments are renounced, knowledge of higher realities and cosmic processes is acquired.

Strong attachments to an illusional sense of Self-identity, erroneous ideas, feelings, pleasant or unpleasant memories, nonuseful behaviors, relationships, places, or things confine our awareness, cloud the mind, and interfere with attempts to imagine and explore higher realities.

When aspiration to be Self- and God-realized is nurtured and commitment to spiritual practice and higher learning does not waver, troublesome attachments are easily renounced.

40. Purity contributes to good health and avoidance of disease.

Being attentive to personal and environmental cleanliness and to the maintenance of a holistic lifestyle is recommended for physical health and well-being. Food and water should be pure, the air that is breathed should be fresh, and the body should be regularly exposed to natural light.

Eating, work, sleep, recreation, metaphysical study, and all other activities should be routinely scheduled, allowing for occasional changes when necessary. Meditation should be regularly practiced to reduce stress, calm the mind, refresh the nervous system, and clarify awareness.

41. The clarity of sattwic influences [in the mind and awareness] contributes to serenity, cheerfulness, purposefulness, mastery of the senses, improved powers of concentration, and receptivity to Self-realization.

We are more receptive to the supportive influences of the elevating attribute of nature when think, live, and act in ways which allow it to be supportive and illuminating.

Doing what contributes to overall well-being and spiritual growth is beneficial. Thoughts, feelings, behaviors, foods, personal and social relationships, and environmental circumstances that are not life-enhancing and that interfere with spiritual growth should be avoided.

42. Contentment provides supreme peace and happiness.

Contentment in all circumstances can be maintained by being Self-aware while dispassionately observing thoughts, feelings, behaviors, and the emergence and disappearance of transitory events.

43. Disciplined purification actions result in perfection of the body, mind, and senses.

The body is purified and refined by wholesome living, nutritious foods, clean environmental conditions, and superconscious influences that flow as we become more spiritually aware. Cleansing procedures can be used to detoxify the body when necessary. The subtle channels through which life forces flow in the spine and brain are purified by pranayama practice and spontaneous movements of kundalini energies that circulate when they have been awakened.

The mind is purified by sattwic influences that are allowed to prevail and by regular practice of superconscious samadhi.

44. Insightful study and analysis of higher realities and intensive spiritual practice result in God-realization.

An intellectual understanding of what God is, what souls are and their origins, and physical and metaphysical laws of cause and effect enables us to know our relationship with God and the universe, live effectively, and meditate skillfully.

45. Self-realization is perfected by devotional surrender to God.

Because we are units of pure consciousness and God is the

cosmic unit of pure consciousness with attributes, surrendering our mistaken sense of Self-identity is the immediate way to awaken to God-realization. All other right endeavors should be known as preparatory practices.

46. The meditation posture should be comfortable and stable.

A poised, upright posture is recommended because it allows attention to be concentrated without being distracted by bodily movements or discomfort. While many meditators prefer to sit in a chair; some like to sit in a cross-legged posture.

47. It [the meditation posture] becomes stable as concentration flows effortlessly and awareness blends with God-consciousness.

This excerpt from the *Bhagavad Gita* (6:10–14) describes the recommended way to meditate.

A practitioner of yoga should steadfastly contemplate the supreme Reality, in solitude, alone, with mind and body controlled, having no cravings for anything.
Established in a comfortable and steady meditation posture, in a clean, appropriate place;
There, intent upon practice, with thoughts and senses controlled, one should engage in meditation to purify the mind.
Holding the body, head, and neck erect, motionless, gazing into the spiritual eye with focused attention;
Serene, fearless, self-controlled, with mental impulses subdued, contemplating the supreme Reality, the devotee should sit, devoted to the highest realization.

48. When obstacles to concentration are removed [or transcended], awareness is released into infinite Consciousness.

Cosmic consciousness and knowledge and experience of the reality of God can then be realized.

49. When the meditation posture is stable, pranayama naturally occurs. Breathing is coordinated and refined, and vital forces flow freely.

At this stage of practice, breathing need not be controlled. When it is slow and refined, mental processes become subtle and less forceful.

50. Modifications of pranayama are external, internal, or still; long, short, or restrained; or regulated by time and number.

During early stages of meditation practice, breathing may be external and forceful, internal and subtle, or may stop for a short duration of time. Forceful breathing confines attention and awareness to the senses and to mental processes. When stress is reduced and the body is relaxed, breathing becomes slow and subtle and mental and emotional calmness prevails.

51. A fourth modification of pranayama neutralizes the inflowing and outflowing breaths.

When the movements of the two aspects of the body's life force which are influential during inhalation and exhalation temporarily stop, superconscious states can be experienced.

During the pauses that naturally occur after inhalation and exhalation, a clear state of awareness can be experienced. By recognizing those brief interludes of clarity, it is possible to assume a clear state of awareness at will. Mastery of attention and of states of consciousness is then acquired.

52. Mastery of that pranayama unveils the reality of the Self.

Self-realization is spontaneously experienced when the mind is calm, subliminal influences are entirely absent, and awareness is clear.

53. It [mastery of that pranayama] allows concentration to flow smoothly.

When the mind is calm, subliminal influences are entirely absent, and awareness is clear, attention is not distracted from the object or ideal being contemplated.

54. Internalization of attention is accomplished by withdrawing it from the senses and directing it inward.

An easy way to internalize attention is to withdraw it from external conditions, then mentally (with feeling) bring it up through the spinal pathway to the front and higher regions of the brain.

55. That [internalization of attention] provides complete mastery of the senses.

When attention is fully inward, there is no perception of external conditions or of physical sensations that might be distracting. Because awareness is then entirely subjective and undistracted, contemplation proceeds without interruption.

CHAPTER THREE

Siddhis

Exceptional Powers of Perception and Extraordinary Abilities

1. An unwavering flow of attention is concentration.

Concentration does not require extreme effort. Direct your attention to what you want to know or with which you want to be identified.

2. Unwavering concentration on the object chosen for contemplation is meditation.

If concentration wavers, focus it by gentle intention or use a meditation technique to more fully involve your attention.

When sitting to meditate, remember why you are doing it and proceed with purposeful intention. It can be helpful to start with prayer to God, as you know or imagine God to be, to invoke God's help and elicit a sense of awareness of God.

3. The self-shining of the object of meditative contemplation is samadhi.

What is realized during samadhi is said to be self-shining (revealed or experienced as it is). There is no awareness of observing anything, only the knowing-experience of what was contemplated is present.

4. Concentration, meditation, and samadhi, together, result in mastery of attention and complete identification of attention and awareness with the object contemplated.

Identification of attention and awareness with an object (light, sound, or any other chosen object), or pure Self-knowledge, may continue until subliminal influences again become active and cause thoughts and feelings to arise. Samadhi of pure Self-knowledge may prevail when thoughts and emotions are present during meditation and at other times.

5. Mastery of meditative contemplation provides insight into what is examined and revelations of higher realities.

In the early stages, insights and perceptions of our true nature and the reality of God may be mixed with erroneous ideas or illusory perceptions. Sustained meditative contemplation results in flawless insights and Self- and God-realization.

6. Meditative contemplation should be practiced in stages.

Two kinds of meditative contemplation can be practiced with benefit. 1) When the mind is calm, contemplate that with which you aspire to be identified until samadhi is established. 2) Contemplate what you want to know until you have insight.

When contemplating to have knowledge revealed, clearly define what you want to know, examine it, and expect to have insight into it. You can then have knowledge of God, your true nature, the categories and processes of cosmic manifestation, or whatever else you desire to know. Insights may at first be unclear or incomplete. When your powers of concentration are developed, you may be pleasantly surprised by the many discoveries that emerge and the abilities that are acquired.

7. These three practices are internal in contrast to the five preceding practices.

Meditative contemplation is subjective. Moral behaviors, intentional disciplines, sitting still, pranayama (regulated or occurring spontaneously) and internalization of attention are preliminary practices that make us receptive to experiencing superconscious states.

8. They [the three practices] become external when samadhi without the support of an object of perception prevails.

When pure superconsciousness is constant, the subjective practices of concentrated meditation and samadhi mixed with thoughts and emotions are transcended.

9. The superior, constructive influences of samadhi overcome and eliminate restrictive subliminal tendencies.

The transformative forces that resist, weaken, and dissolve harmful subconscious conditions while attention is absorbed in pure superconsciousness continue to be influential after a meditation practice session.

As the mind and intellect are purified, episodes of cosmic consciousness that provide knowledge of the wholeness of life are increasingly experienced during meditation and while we are engaged in normal activities.

10. The serene, transformative flow [of superconscious influences] that occurs is due to its innate purity.

Transformative superconscious influences, being entirely sattwic or pure, easily dominate and progressively overcome rajasic and tamasic influences in the mind and body.

11. When attention and awareness are absorbed in that samadhi, all sense of otherness disappears.

When the illusional (mistaken) sense of Self is transcended, pure existence-being is realized.

12. When concentration is focused, sequential ideas that arise in the mind are similar.

Similar, sequential thoughts that arise in the mind when attention is focused can be objectively observed until they subside or they can be carefully examined for the purpose of acquiring useful insights.

When aspiring to be Self-realized, observe streams of thoughts until they can be ignored. When contemplating that which you aspire to know, let thoughts continue until they are replaced by intellectual or intuitive insights or by Self-revealed knowledge.

13. The varieties and characteristics of changes that occur in the mind and body are thus known.

Accurate understanding of mental processes is acquired by calm observation of their actions. Impressions of perceptions that are processed by the mind enable us to recall our past perceptions, thoughts, and experiences; retain memories of what is now being perceived, thought, and experienced; and wisely use our knowledge. Mental processes which enable us to function effectively in time and space are transcended during meditative, pure superconsciousness and are helpful to us when we are engaged in everyday activities.

14. The deeper levels of consciousness have conditions which may be dormant, aroused, or have potential for manifestation that is not yet predictable.

Dormant impressions that modify the mind and awareness may be activated and become influential or may be dissolved by superconscious influences. Influences which are present to be observed can be allowed to be expressive if they are supportive, or resisted and overcome if they are harmful. The possible influences of conditions which have potential to be expressive will be known and can be effectively related to as they become activated, or be resisted and dissolved by making wise choices and nurturing superconsciousness.

15. The orders, relationships, and arrangements of subliminal impressions determine their influential effects.

The kinds and characteristics of mental conditionings and how they are related and organized in the mind determine their possible influences.

Karmic patterns which are similar are more influential because of their related or combined inclinations. Traumatic and pleasurable events, and clearly defined desires driven by emotion or nourished by aspiration, make strong impressions in the mind. Insignificant events, unclearly defined desires, and random hopes make weak impressions.

Physical weakness, mental confusion, emotional unrest, indecisiveness, laziness, and complacency make it difficult to resist and overcome karmic influences.

16. Meditative contemplation on the three kinds of subliminal influences provides knowledge of one's past and [possible] future.

Insights into karmic conditions which are dormant, active, or have potential to be influential may bring forth memories of previous experiences and provide knowledge of what may be experienced in the near or distant future if they are not neutralized, dissolved, or transcended.

A fatalistic attitude regarding karmic influences should be avoided. Because they are only impressions in the mind, they cannot dominate our thinking, feeling, or behaviors when we are Self-determined and wisely purposeful.

Karmic influences which might cause unwanted effects if allowed to be expressive can often be transmuted (changed) into constructive influences by optimistic thinking and feeling, soul-inspired, purpose-driven actions, and regular, sustained, superconscious meditation practice.

17. Words, ideas, and feelings are often mixed and confused. By insightful analysis of their distinctions, knowledge of sounds made by people and creatures can be acquired.

The meaning of what a person is endeavoring to verbally communicate can often be known by sensing their mental and emotional state and observing their behaviors and manner of speaking: the tone and pitch of their voice and other sounds they make (irrelevant words, sighs, gasps, grunts, or groans). What they do not say is often more revealing that what is said. It can also be helpful to intuitively discern their intentions.

The kinds, and characteristics, of sounds made by animals and other creatures (and their behaviors) also communicate desires, needs, and intentions which can be known when we are attentive.

18. By directly perceiving subliminal impressions, knowledge of previous incarnations may be acquired.

Although memories of former astral, causal, or physical life-cycles *may* be elicited, having knowledge of them that is vivid and accurate is not commonly experienced. During the phase of transition from one realm to another, awareness may be temporarily blurred or fragmented and memories may be suppressed. If what seem to be clear memories of previous incarnations are helpful, make the most of what is known (or is thought to be known). It is not spiritually useful, however, to be preoccupied with endeavors to remember past events or to indulge in fantasies about them. It is more beneficial to live effectively, acquire higher knowledge, and fulfill our spiritual destiny by doing what can be done now to allow our innate, divine qualities to emerge and be actualized.

19. By understanding the operations of the mind and awareness, knowledge of the mental states and states of awareness of others can be acquired.

By knowing how the mind processes perceptions that are reflected to it by awareness of what is perceived, the mental states and states of awareness of others can be known.

20. Knowing the contents of another person's mind and awareness does not support those states because the intent is to have insight rather than to identify with what is known.

The contents of another person's mind and their states of

awareness are related to their perceptions and their reactions or responses to what is perceived. Our knowledge does not influence their mental states and states of awareness (except when the unique circumstances described in sutra 39 of this chapter exist).

21. By preventing [ordinary] light from being reflected from the physical body, one becomes invisible to others.

Visual perception of objects occurs when electromagnetic waves (of visible light) are reflected from them to our eyes and electrical impulses are transmitted to optic centers in the brain. If light is not reflected from an object, it is not perceived.

22. The disappearance [of perception] of sound, taste, touch, smell, and hearing is thus explained.

We do not ordinarily perceive what is not communicated to our mind and consciousness by one or more of our five senses. Extrasensory powers of intuition can be used to know what cannot be perceived through the physical senses.

23. By contemplation on karmic influences which are slow or fast in producing effects, knowledge of the causes of one's death, or that of others, and other unusual occurrences can be acquired.

Subliminal conditions that influence mental attitudes and personal behaviors that weaken the body's immune system, contribute to illness or disease, or to accident-prone or erratic behaviors, can provide indications of how and when a person may leave this world.

Premature death of the body should be avoided. Healthy, long life lived with conscious intention provides opportunities for accomplishing our major purposes, including the ultimate purpose for our being in this realm—to fully awaken to Self- and God-realization.

When misfortune is personally experienced or observed, it is not uncommon to hear someone say, "Why did it have to happen?" "It doesn't make any sense." "Why does God allow such things to happen to me (or to others)?"

When we know the inner causes of outer effects and that mental states and personal behaviors tend to produce results which correspond to them, we are not inclined to question why events occur.

God does not cause misfortune, distress, or suffering, nor does an evil force exist that can produce hardship. For every event that occurs, there is hidden or an obvious cause that can be discovered. By knowing the causes of events, those that may contribute to unwanted circumstances can be changed or their effects avoided.

24. Mental, moral, and spiritual strength is acquired by meditative contemplation on friendliness, compassion, and other virtues.

To be more mentally competent, "see" yourself as being mentally competent, be alert and attentive, think rationally, and improve your powers of concentration and discriminative intelligence. To be more virtuous, assume a virtuous mental attitude and the behaviors which correspond to it. To be spiritually strong (established in Self-knowledge and wisely purposeful), acknowledge the truth of what you are as a unit of supreme Consciousness and live your immortal life with that understanding.

25. Contemplation on various kinds of power empowers one.

To have the capacity to think and act effectively, actualize your capacity to do what you want to do by wisely using your knowledge and skills to acquire more skills and increasing your capacity to think and act effectively.

26. By projecting attention and awareness into the cosmic field of supreme Consciousness, that which is veiled, subtle, or remote can be known.

When attention and awareness merge with supreme Consciousness, knowledge of its attributes and processes can be apprehended. Meditative contemplation on inner light and sound expands our awareness and provides perceptions of omnipresence and omniscience.

27. Contemplation on the sun provides knowledge of celestial bodies and categories and processes of cosmic manifestation.

Examination of the origin and structure of the universe can begin by acquiring available knowledge from a variety of reliable sources and proceed to metaphysical studies of facts that are known and theories that are well-reasoned. The final stage is to calmly, thoughtfully, and intuitively contemplate the source, causes, categories, and processes of a universe.

A sun's radiation energizes the realm of space that it influences. The supreme, ultimate Sun is the Cosmic Soul (God) from which forces emanate that produce, enliven, and maintain a universe. Our understanding of the cosmos is not complete until knowledge of that which makes all things possible, our relationship to it, and the categories and processes of cosmic manifestation, is flawless.

28. Contemplation on the moon and planets provides knowledge of their relationships and movements.
29. Contemplation on the Pole Star provides knowledge of the relationships and movements of stars [suns].

See *yuga* in the glossary.

30. Contemplation on the central nervous system provides knowledge of it and other systems of the body.

Before endeavoring to meditatively acquire knowledge of the body's systems, the perusal of books and other sources of valid information regarding the biological science of essential and typical life processes and functions is recommended as a practical approach to discovery.

Physical processes and functions are influenced by three cosmic governing principles which pervade all of nature and influence all living things. See *ayurveda* in the glossary.

31. Regulation of appetite and thirst provides mastery of them.

A balanced low-calorie, nutrition-rich, vegetarian diet that is compatible with a person's basic mind-body constitution is recommended. Overeating should be avoided. An ideal body weight should be maintained.

Life forces that flow from our essence of being into the physical body through the medulla oblongata at the base of brain and circulate throughout the body can be consciously directed to muscles, organs, and systems to vitalize them.

Some yogis can, by concentrating at the medulla and the chakra opposite the throat, and by using a certain pranayama technique, absorb fine cosmic forces that nourish the body and reduce the need for food and water.

32. Contemplation on the center of equilibrium in the chest produces steadiness of states of consciousness.

In the early stages of meditation before a superconscious state is established, being simultaneously aware at the dorsal, cervical, spiritual eye, and crown chakra will keep attention and awareness grounded and focused.

Doing this when engaged in ordinary activities encourages an upward flow of life forces, keeps awareness clear, enables us to be even-minded, and contributes to emotional stability.

33. By contemplating the light at the crown chakra, awakened souls have direct perception of Reality.

With attention and awareness established in the higher brain when meditating, extend your awareness a few inches above your head. If you hear a constant flow of subtle sound, consider it to be an aspect of the Om vibration and float your awareness in it. If a sound-frequency does not manifest, sit in the deep silence.

Poised and still, patiently observe with calm anticipation and gentle, sustained aspiration to awaken to a pure-conscious state.

34. From the flash of perception [that occurs] knowledge of ultimate Reality blossoms.

Sustained meditative contemplation, patiently waiting and watching with aspiration to know the full reality of supreme Consciousness, allows innate knowledge of it to emerge. If illuminating perceptions do not immediately occur, continue to contemplate with alert anticipation. If insights are not had when meditating, they may occur at other times when you are calm and alert.

35. Contemplation on the heart [one's essence of being] provides all knowledge of it.

The direct way to be Self-realized is to meditatively aspire to experience your pure-conscious essence. Inquire, "What am I?" Doing this does not require active thinking, although thoughts may arise during the early stages. Calmly desire to know and vividly experience what you really are.

You know that you are not the mind, the contents of which you can observe. You know you are not the physical body which was born and will die. You are a seer, an observer and knower. Patient, alert contemplation of your true nature will eventually result in an adjustment of viewpoint that allows you to be Self-realized. Self-knowing may occur gradually or it may be sudden, and may be partial or complete.

36. Realization of one's essence of being provides knowledge of the difference between it and ordinary states of awareness.

When you know what you are as a spiritual being, you are removed from the influences of modified states of awareness. The difference between what you are and modified states of awareness can be discerned by using your powers of discriminative intelligence and improved powers of intuition.

37. From that superior realization, exceptional powers of perception and extraordinary abilities result.

It is natural for a person who is spiritually conscious to have these powers and abilities which many people who are not yet spiritually awake consider to be exceptional.

38. When used only for external purposes, they become obstacles to the accomplishment of higher samadhi. They should primarily be used to weaken and remove harmful subliminal tendencies.

Using these powers and abilities only to fulfill mundane purposes or to satisfy ego-motivated desires interferes with spiritual growth. They can, however, be wisely used to enhance everyday circumstances and superconscious meditation practice.

39. By focused concentration, one can enter [identify with] the mind and body of another person.

Identifying with the mind of another person enables us to know its condition, and when appropriate and permissible, to constructively influence it. The best way to assist others is to share your realization of wholeness with them. Endeavors to mentally control, or harm, others with thoughts or will power should be avoided.

40. Mastery of the upward-flowing aspect of prana enables one to avoid contact with harmful conditions in nature and to leave the body consciously at the time of transition.

Five aspects of life force are expressive in the physical body. When the influence of the upward flowing aspect of life force prevails, a feeling of lightness is sensed, awareness is inclined to be identified with the higher chakras and their characteristics, and superconsciousness is easier to maintain.

When transition from the body is inevitable, a spiritually aware person can choose to depart by raising their life forces through the central channel in the spine to the crown chakra.

41. Mastery of the aspect of prana that regulates body chemistry contributes to radiant physical well-being.

The influences of this aspect of prana, seated in the stomach and intestines, are increased by enlivening the solar plexus and lumbar chakra, keeping the mind-body constitution balanced (with foods, exercise, stress management, appropriate exercise, a hatha yoga practice [*uddiyana bandha*] that affects the abdominal region), and inspired, enthusiastic, purposeful living.

42. By meditative contemplation on ether-space, subtle sounds can be heard.

Subtle sounds that are heard should be listened to until a continuously flowing sound that can be used as a meditation mantra is heard.

43. Contemplation on the relationship between the body and space, with the idea of lightness, may result in levitation.

Although levitation of the body is (perhaps) possible, this should not be of primary importance to one who aspires to be spiritually enlightened. It is of greater value to acquire the ability to "elevate" attention and awareness: to remove it from mundane influences which might interfere with awakening to Self- and God-realization.

44. Contemplation on states beyond gross modifications of the mind unveils the coverings that confine the Self.

Preoccupation with the contents of the mind during meditation practice keeps attention involved with them. Meditative contemplation on higher realities allows them to be realized.

45. Contemplation of gross matter, its essential attributes and components and their subtle aspects and drives, provides mastery over its energies and forces.

In the current era, we are becoming increasingly aware of the many scientific and technological discoveries being made by individuals who use exceptional powers of intellect, imagination, and intuition to investigate the finer attributes of matter and use their knowledge for practical, beneficial purposes.

Dedicated truth seekers are spiritual scientists whose discoveries enable them to live effectively and awaken from all delusions and illusions.

46. Because of the superior knowledge that is acquired, and its wise use, exceptional powers of perception become pronounced and the body becomes strong and healthy.

Improvement of powers of perception and overall health and well-being indicate that spiritual growth is authentic. It is impossible to experience real spiritual growth without having some outward signs of improvement of functional powers and physical and circumstantial conditions.

Many people study metaphysical themes for years without having insight, assuming responsibility for their thoughts and actions, or meditating superconsciously. They remain confined to their illusional states of awareness, consider themselves to be victims of karma or of external conditions, pray with faint hope for results, meditate passively, and falsely presume that they are intent on a spiritual path.

Intentional, right spiritual practice produces results that are obvious to the practitioner.

47. Some characteristics of physical perfection are gracefulness, bright complexion, vitality, and adamantine hardness.

The word *adamantine* (diamond-like) is used to indicate the durability of a healthy body with a strong immune system.

48. Contemplation on the senses, their powers, characteristics, and purposes provides mastery of the senses.

The five senses convey information to the mind where it is

processed and organized. We are superior to the senses, mind, and faculty of intellect we use to interpret and define what is sensed and thought.

49. By knowing the distinction between the attributes of nature and the Self and by mastering the senses, supremacy over all states of consciousness is acquired.

When Self-knowledge is constant, we can remain stable in that realization while observing our feelings and thoughts and perceiving objective phenomena through the five senses. Our feelings, thoughts, and senses are then effortlessly controlled.

50. By discriminative contemplation on the distinction between the illuminating attribute of nature and the true Self, perceptions of omnipresence and omniscience are experienced.

When attention is completely withdrawn from subliminal rajasic and tamasic influences, awareness reflects the purity of the influences of sattwa guna. When attention is removed from that, awareness expands and knowledge that pervades infinite Consciousness becomes accessible.

51. When there are no attachments to superconscious states or to perceptions of omnipotence or omniscience, and all traces of subliminal restrictions have been dissolved, pure Self-realization prevails.

Attachments to superconscious experiences or to intuitive perceptions of higher realities confine awareness and sustain a mistaken sense of independent Self-identity. They may be erroneously thought of as indications of the ultimate stage of spiritual growth or be attractive because of the enjoyment that is experienced. When attachments of this kind have been renounced and the mind and awareness have been cleansed of all modifying influences, the final stage of soul awakening is effortlessly actualized.

52. Upon awakening to Self-knowledge there must be no sense of pride of attainment or attachments to prior conditions, as this can result in a return to former states of consciousness.

Obvious or subtle thoughts or feelings of pride about what has been accomplished by our endeavors, or attachments to memories of insightful perceptions that preceded it, should be avoided. Attention should remain anchored in Self-knowledge until that realization is flawless and permanent.

53. By contemplation on moments of time and their progressions, discriminative knowledge of time is acquired.

Time, commonly thought of as intervals between events that occur, is a component of a continuum (wholeness) which includes space and cosmic forces, no part of which can be objectively distinguished from others except by evaluation for the purpose of analysis or theoretical speculation. When our awareness of the contents of the primordial field of nature is improved, the component aspects of that field can be known.

54. With that knowledge, one can discern the distinction between similar events which have characteristics that cannot be otherwise determined.

If we are not capable of discerning with accuracy, we may mistakenly presume that similar events that occur at different intervals of time have identical causes. What occurs at any moment is unique because it corresponds to its specific cause.

55. Flawless, discriminative knowledge simultaneously includes knowledge of all aspects of what is perceived.

If powers of discernment are not highly developed, only partial knowledge of what is examined can be apprehended. Total knowledge of what is contemplated may be intuitively perceived or be experienced as a sudden revelation. Intuitive perceptions have an object, something at which one looks or which is contemplated. Intuitive knowledge of relative things or circumstances is accurate at the moment of knowing. When examined later, the condition or circumstance that was formerly examined may be different because change is always occurring in the relative realms which extend from the field of primordial nature to a material universe.

Revelations that provide complete knowledge of higher realities emerge from our consciousness where all knowledge of what is permanently real exists.

56. When the purity of the Self, mind, intellect, and awareness is the same, absolute Self-knowledge prevails.

Only a portion of an ego-confined soul's awareness is identified with mental characteristics which modify it. When it is entirely clarified, pure Self-realization is constant.

CHAPTER FOUR

Liberation of Consciousness

The Culmination of Right Practice

1. Exceptional powers of perception and extraordinary abilities result from superconscious samadhi which may be experienced because of circumstances at one's birth, wise use of herbs or mantras, or intensity of spiritual practice.

Circumstances related to one's birth include the degree of spiritual awareness when born, karmic influences, one's basic mind-body constitution, and environmental factors. Although some souls are more spiritually aware than others and have functional capacities that can be quickly actualized, all souls have the same potential to awaken to Self-realization.

Wise use of nutritious foods and herbs can beneficially influence biochemical processes and contribute to physical health, mental acuity, and clarity of awareness.

Use of a meditation mantra improves concentration, calms the mind, and pacifies subliminal influences.

Intensive kriya yoga practice elicits superconscious states.

2. Transformation of the senses, mind, and body occurs because of flows of natural forces.

Free-flowing life forces purify the mind, refine the brain, and enliven the nervous system, allowing our consciousness to be more easily expressive through the mind and body.

Dormant soul forces (kundalini energies) awakened by devotion, fervent aspiration to be Self-realized, spiritual practices, and superconscious influences are extremely transformative. Spontaneous kundalini awakening may also occur because of sustained mental and spiritual attunement with someone who is already spiritually awake and by being in an environment that is sanctified (holy, pure) because of the devotion, prayer, and spiritual practices of others.

3. Intensive spiritual practices remove obstacles that inhibit flows of transformative forces.

Dedicated, intensive spiritual practice makes us receptive to flows of transformative forces that arise from within us. When these forces can flow freely, psychological and physical transformations occur effortlessly. When they freely flow and a balanced, wholesome, and supportive lifestyle is maintained, spiritual awakening proceeds smoothly and quickly.

4. Individualized units of consciousness are produced by one, supreme Consciousness.

Because all units of one, supreme Consciousness have the same attributes and innate knowledge as that Reality, the actualization of these qualities and capacities is not a condition to be attained; it is the natural result of progressive spiritual awakening that unveils our innate qualities and knowledge and restores our awareness to wholeness.

5. Although individualized units of consciousness have different relationships with the realm of nature, they are impelled by one, supreme Consciousness.

The relationships we have with the world and with others with whom we interact are determined by karmic influences, our mental states and states of awareness, our desires and actions, and the choices we make. The impulses of supreme Consciousness that enliven and empower the processes that occur in nature also enliven and empower us.

6. Of the modifications of awareness, those produced by samadhi
    are devoid of karmic influences.

Mental impressions made by superconscious experiences do
not compel our actions or produce external effects; they weaken
and dissolve harmful karmic tendencies which, when removed,
allow us to more freely express and to more easily meditate.

7. Restrained modifications of awareness are neither construc-
    tive nor destructive. Others are of three kinds.

Awareness-modifying influences that are inhibited cannot
cause effects. Those which are not restrained may influence
thoughts, emotions, and behaviors in ways that may either
enhance our lives or cause discomfort. If they are not permanently restrained and dissolved, they may be activated in the
near or distant future.

8. The forces of karma become influential when conditions most
    suitable for their expression exist.

Subliminal conditions which have potential to influence
thoughts, feelings, and behaviors may be activated by similar
thoughts, feelings, behaviors, and our responses or reactions to
events that we observe or experience.

9. Because of the similarity of thoughts and memories, feelings
    may be aroused with memories even though they are sepa-
    rated by space and time.

When we are reminded of an event that occurred in the near
or distant past, it is not uncommon to also experience the feelings that resulted from observation or experience of that event.
Memories of similar events or experiences that are not directly
related to what is presently perceived may bring forth feelings of
discomfort or mental confusion. Such discomfort or confusion can
be avoided by remaining calm and maintaining a mental attitude of dispassionate objectivity.

10. Because of the innate urge of supreme Consciousness to express, there is no moment of time that can be determined regarding the flow of causes and their effects.

No precise moment of time can be determined regarding the beginning of the emanation of the vibration of the power of Consciousness that causes a universe to manifest, because that event preceded the appearance of time in the primordial field of nature. Because the urge of supreme Consciousness to express in, and as, nature is omnipresently expressive, when and where its impulses that cause effects to arise defy detection.

11. Karmic influences exist because of a mistaken sense of Self and the support of objects of perception. In their absence, karmic influences disappear.

When we are Self-knowing, illusions are absent because we do not misinterpret what is observed. Karma accumulated because of relationships with relative phenomena cannot be influential when awareness is removed from it.
When attention and awareness are absorbed in a pure superconscious state, karmic influences are transcended.

12. Subliminal impressions and memories of past perceptions of events exist with the potential for future events to occur. How future events unfold is determined by one's path in life.

The future experiences of individuals who have similar karmic conditions may differ because of their different mental states and states of awareness, the choices they make, and the actions they perform to fulfill their aspirations.
The experiences and circumstances of a person whose awareness and interests are ordinary are much different than those of a person who aspires to Self-realization and adheres to a regimen of wholesome living and spiritual practice.

13. Karmic conditions are empowered by the influences of the three constituent attributes of nature.

The influences of some karmic conditions are life-enhancing; some cause mental and emotional unrest and stimulate the senses; some dull the mind and cloud awareness. Tamasic influences that dull the mind and cloud awareness can be resisted and their forces transformed by cultivating optimism and engaging in purposeful actions.

Rajasic influences that cause mental and emotional unrest and stimulate the senses can be resisted and overcome by nurturing peace of mind and emotional stability, orderly behaviors, and superconsciousness. Sattwic influences should be allowed to be influential.

14. Because of unified interactions of the three attributes of nature that are influential regarding karmic conditions, there is a unity of manifestations of events and circumstances.

Outer, objective effects correspond with inner, subjective causes. By apprehending the wholeness of life, instead of thinking of life in terms of divisions and parts, our cosmic conscious perceptions enable us to know that all things from the pure field of Consciousness to the material realm are interrelated and to discern the relationships between subtle causes and their obvious effects.

15. Because of the differences of units of consciousness, objects are perceived differently and the life-path of each unit is different.

Because the karmic conditions, mental states, intellectual capacities, functional skills, aspirations, and levels of spiritual awareness of individuals are different, no two people have the same perceptions of the world and their relationship to it. Nor do they have the same life-path, although all have the same spiritual destiny.

16. The existence of a material object is not dependent upon the perception of an observer.

A universe is not an illusion, although our misperceptions of it may be illusory. When spiritually enlightened people say the world is unreal, they mean that it does not exist apart from that which produced and sustains it.

17. How an observed object is perceived is determined by the powers of perception of the observer.

Flawed or weak powers of perception result in inaccurate or incomplete knowledge. Acute powers of perception provide accurate knowledge of what is observed.

18. Because the true Self is changeless, all of the modifications of its awareness are known by it.

When we are established in Self-knowing, the contents of our mind and awareness can be known. As units of one field of Reality, we are not affected by transformations that occur in our mind and awareness.

19. Individual awareness is not self-luminous; it is illumined by the radiance of the Self.

Awareness reflects objects of perception; it can only be illumined when it reflects the purity of our essence of being.

20. Because awareness is not self-luminous, it cannot simultaneously reflect the reality of the Self and objective conditions.

Pure samadhi cannot be experienced while our awareness is reflecting perceptions of external conditions. When pure samadhi prevails, there is no perception of outer conditions.

We can, however, be Self-knowing and observe objective phenomena when we are not meditating, while awareness is reflecting to our mind what is presented to it.

21. If the contents of the minds of all units of consciousness were intermingled, memories would be confused.

Our memories and streams of thoughts provide us with a unique sense of self-identity and knowledge of our history in space and time.

22. The changeless unit of consciousness acquires a faculty of intellect when it identifies with fine matter.

When units of pure consciousness become involved with primordial nature and become egocentric, the faculty of intellect that is acquired enables them to examine and comprehend what is perceived. Souls with weak powers of discrimination erroneously presume their illusional sense of Self-identity to be their real nature.

23. Individualized consciousness is modified by what is observed.

When powers of discrimination are weak and awareness is blurred, what is seen, felt, and thought about further clouds the mind and consciousness.

24. The mind, with its various driving forces, exists to serve the Self.

A mind receives, records, and processes information. The forces that express through the mind are 1) instinctive urges that impel us to survive and express; 2) soul force embedded with mental impressions that have potential to be influential (karma); 3) the influences of the three gunas; 4) the power of our will or intention which may be constructive or otherwise. What is sometimes described as "mind power" is the power of will or intention expressed through the mind.

A well-ordered mind enables us to think rationally and to effectively relate to our world.

25. The mistaken sense of Self disappears when the distinction between modified states of awareness, the influences of sattwa guna, and one's pure-conscious essence is seen.

The distinction between our essence, and what we are not, can be either intellectually discerned, intuitively known, or actually realized. Intellectual discernment can provide partial understanding; intuition can provide insight; actual realization provides comprehensive knowledge.

26. Awareness is then inclined to serenely flow in the direction of absolute freedom.

When awareness is no longer confined by erroneous ideas or illusions, it is attracted to that which will illumine it. Progressive awakening to the final stage of liberation of consciousness then occurs easily and quickly.

27. Even when awareness is inclined in the direction of liberation, interruptions of that flow may occur when the mind and awareness are disturbed by subliminal tendencies.

Subliminal tendencies that were weakened and quieted, but not completely neutralized, may occasionally be aroused and activate thoughts and emotions which distract attention.

28. Subliminal tendencies should be returned to a dormant state.

Thoughts and emotions which are activated by subliminal influences during interludes of meditative contemplation can be passively disregarded while concentration remains focused and gentle aspiration to be fully awake is sustained. Even if interesting visions or other subtle, pleasant perceptions are had, they should be ignored and transcended.

29. When distinctions between sattwic influences and one's pure consciousness is constantly discerned and one has no self-interest regarding higher states of realization, pure samadhi can be experienced.

Realization of our pure-conscious essence is not caused by any external influence; it is actualized when nothing external is influential. Being concerned about how higher realizations may affect us disturbs concentration, sustains a false sense of Self-identity, and inhibits spiritual awakening. Aspiration to liberation of consciousness supports meditative contemplation and improves receptivity to samadhi.

30. With the emergence of Self-knowing, all karmic conditions cease to be influential.

When Self-realization prevails during meditation practice, subliminal tendencies are dormant. When Self-realization is constant after meditation, troublesome subliminal tendencies are easily resisted, dissolved by superconscious influences, or discarded because of our higher understanding.

31. Then, because of the superior knowledge which has removed the residues of karma from the mind, very little remains to be known.

When all traces of troublesome subliminal impressions are gone, knowledge of higher realities and the processes of life is easily acquired or emerges from within the essence of our being.

32. Because of that, the influences of the attributes of nature, having accomplished their purposes, cease to be influential.

The influences of rajas guna help us overcome tamasic influences, contribute to psychological transformation, and assist us in the performance of intensive spiritual practices. The influences of sattwa guna purify the mind and clarify awareness. When we are spiritually enlightened, the support of these attributes of nature is no longer required.

33. Sequential progression of transformations that occur moment to moment can be apprehended at the final end of their changes.

As samadhi states become refined, the subtle changes that occur from stage to stage can be discerned by the meditator.

34. Liberation of consciousness is realized when the attributes of nature that have been restored to their primary state are devoid of influences and the Self is established in its own essence of being.

When the three attributes of nature are restored to a state of equilibrium and are inactive, absolute freedom prevails.

The Sanskrit word that describes this freedom is *kaivalya,* "isolation"— "the aloneness of seeing clearly." To be isolated is to be set apart from external influences. When we are thus free, our Self-knowing is constant and our perceptions are flawless.

35. Liberation of consciousness is then complete.

There are two stages of liberation of consciousness. At the first stage, Self-realization is not flawless and a residue of causative conditions in the mind has to be discarded, dissolved, or transcended. The final stages are described as follows:

36. The liberated Self abides in pure consciousness.

Self-realization is permanent when it is impervious to all consciousness-modifying influences.

37. One Reality is then known and the universe and its processes are seen as self-referring actions of that Reality.

Along with flawless Self-realization, innate knowledge of one Reality and its processes emerges and blossoms.

38. The characteristics of the expressive aspect of that Reality are consciousness, existence, and bliss. Its absolute aspect is devoid of attributes.

When our Self-realization blossoms into God-realization, we are continuously conscious, aware of existing beyond time and space, and experience the pure joy of being.

Beyond realization of God and God's attributes is flawless realization of pure existence-being.

PART TWO

The Shandilya Upanishad

The Inner Meaning of the Bhagavad Gita

Preface

upanishad From the Sanskrit verb-root *sad* (to sit) with the prefixes *upa* (near) and *ni* (down). A treatise on spiritual and philosophical subjects usually presented as though the student were "sitting near" the teacher to learn.

At least two hundred Upanishads are known; orthodox tradition puts their number at one hundred and eight. Composed for the most part by anonymous authors, they represent the philosophical systems of Vedanta: the culmination of the teachings of the Vedas (knowledge of higher realities said to have been revealed to ancient sages). For hundreds of years before the invention of the printing press, the Upanishads were transmitted orally from teachers to students. A few Persian translations were published in the fifteenth century and then into Latin in 1801. The first English translations of some of the Upanishads were published in 1832.

The better known Upanishads about which commentaries were written by Shankara, the eighth century Indian philosopher-seer, and others, are considered to be the principle ones for ordinary truth seekers. The Shandilya Upanishad is assigned to the category of "Yoga Upanishads" in which esoteric information is meant for devotees who are presumed to be morally, intellectually, and spiritually prepared to receive and benefit by it. In the text, Shandilya is portrayed as an attentive disciple who asks his teacher Atharvan to provide knowledge of higher realities which will satisfy the mind and for guidance in spiritual practice which will free the spirit (soul).

Babajji told Lahiri Mahasaya that one of Lahiri's ancestors had written the Shandilya Upanishad. The philosophical concepts and practices described in it are those of this kriya yoga tradition. Complicated sentences are rephrased and some duplication of material is omitted. To make reading and comprehension easier, most of the Sanskrit words are replaced with equivalent English meanings without diluting the potency of the teachings. *Italics* are used when a word is defined or explained.

CHAPTER FIVE

The Shandilya Upaniṣhad

Shandilya asked:

Please tell me about the eight parts of yoga: the means by which Self-realization may be accomplished.

Artharvan replied:

The moral and ethical observances [*yamas*, restraints]; the required disciplined practices or intentional actions [*niyamas*]; postures [*asanas*]; mastery of life force [*pranayama*]; detachment of awareness from the senses and internalization of attention [*pratyahara*]; alert concentration [*dharana*], meditation [*dhyana*], and *samadhi* [realization of oneness]. There are ten moral and ethical observances, ten disciplined practices; eight meditation postures; three kinds of pranayama; five stages of internalization of attention and of concentration; two kinds of meditation; and one kind of samadhi.

Commentary:

Ashtanga (eight-limbed) yoga practice, also referred to as raja yoga, is described. Ten each of the moral and ethical observances and the disciplined practices are mentioned in contrast to five of each which are mentioned in Patanjali's yoga-sutras. There is no rigid rule in regard to teaching these principles. So long as the basic information is imparted, the teacher may present it however it may seem to be appropriate. The kinds and methods of pranayama and other practices are determined by the teacher in accord with what is thought to be best for the disciple. There is only "one kind of samadhi" (identification of awareness with an object of meditative contemplation); preliminary samadhi states are supported by an object of contemplation.

Text:

The moral and ethical guidelines are these. 1) Harmlessness in thought, speech, and action. 2) Truthfulness, which is conducive to well-being. 3) Refraining from coveting that which belongs to others. 4) Conservation and transmutation of vital forces. 5) Kindliness toward all creatures. 6) Equanimity during the performance of dutiful actions and the nonperformance of forbidden actions. 7) Patience in all circumstances. 8) Mental stability during the gain or loss of wealth or relationships. 9) Appropriate choices of nutritious foods. 10) Purity. External purity is of the body; internal purity is of the mind and is accomplished by psychological transformation and Self-realization.

Commentary:

The yoga-sutras recommend the cultivation of harmlessness; truthfulness; honesty; conservation and transmutation of vital forces; and noncovetousness by power of will (decisive choice), self-control, and replacement of destructive tendencies with constructive mental attitudes and actions.

Text:

The disciplines. 1) Liberating the mind and body from all limitations by self-analysis and regulated behaviors. 2) Satisfaction with what life spontaneously provides [when it is supportive]. 3) Acknowledgment of the laws of cause and effect. 4) Giving lawfully earned or acquired resources to deserving people and worthy causes. 5) Worship of God with pure motives in accord with one's understanding. 6) Inquiring into the meaning of scriptures. 7) Remorse for behavior that is contrary to scriptural or social rules. 8) Faith in one's spiritual path. 9) Using mantras received from the guru. 10) Regularity of performance of these practices [and avoidance of those which are contrary to them].

Commentary:

In the yoga-sutras the recommended practices are cleanliness; the cultivation of soul contentment; mastery of mental and sensory impulses; metaphysical study; and complete surrender to God (renunciation of the illusional sense of selfhood). Mantra practice is of two kinds: audible chanting and mental listening while contemplating its essence. Audible chanting is of value; mental listening is said to produce superior results.

Text:

Let the person who is unable to use all of the postures adopt any of them which may be found to be easy and pleasant. One who masters the postures acquires dominion over the three worlds. Established in the moral and ethical observances and the disciplined practices, one should practice pranayama, for by it all of the *nadis* [channels through which life forces flow] are purified.

Commentary:

The text describes eight seated meditation postures which should be "easy and pleasant" so that concentration will not be disturbed. The two classic meditation postures for poise and balance are *padmasana* (lotus posture) and *siddhasana* (posture of one whose contemplation is "perfected" or accomplished or who is aspiring to spiritual perfection); the latter is more comfortable than the lotus posture. Sitting upright in a comfortable chair is usually more suitable for devotees who are not accustomed to using a cross-legged posture and is permissible. The "three worlds" over which to have dominion are unconscious, subconscious, and ordinary waking states.

Shandilya:

By what means are the nadis purified? How many are in the body? How do they arise and what vital airs are located in them? What are their seats [primary locations] and functions? Whatever in the body is worthy of being known, please tell me.

Artharvan:

Prana [life force] extends [radiates an aura] approximately six inches from the body. One who by practice of yoga reduces the prana in the body to make it equal to or not less than the fire in it, becomes an exceptional yoga practitioner. The region of fire, triangular in form and brilliant as molten gold, is located in the middle of the body as a chakra with ten radiations of life force. Influenced by the unbalanced energies of this chakra, the soul wanders, driven by its karma. In the physical body, the soul rides upon prana. At the base of the sushumna is the seat of kundalini. Its actions are restrained because of the soul's involvement with objective circumstances and closes the opening of the brahmarandra. During the practice of yoga it is awakened by the fire and shines with great brilliancy in the space of the heart in the form of wisdom. Fourteen principle nadis are the major conduits for the flow of kundalini shakti. Of them, sushumna is said to be the sustainer of the universe and the path of salvation. It extends from the base of the spine to the brahmarandra at the top of the head, is subtle, and has enlivening and preservative influences. On the left side of sushumna is ida; on the right side is pingala. Ida, of the nature of the moon, is tamasic. Pingala, of the nature of the sun, is rajasic. They indicate time, of which sushumna is the consumer. Other nadis extend from the spinal pathway throughout the body. As a tree leaf is covered with minute fibers, so also is this body permeated with nadis.

Commentary:

To reduce the life force in the body to "make it equal to or not less than the fire in it" is to maintain a balance of the actions of life force. When life forces are either aggravated and excessive in their actions or their influences are weak or insufficient, psychological and physical disturbance may result. Yoga practitioners are advised to adapt ayurvedic regimens to their personal needs to restore and maintain balanced flows of life force.

The vital center at the lumbar region of the spine is said to have ten aspects of life force influence. The "triangular form" of life force manifestation in this chakra is said to be manifested by its unique energy frequencies. Visualizing a specific form of life force manifestation in a chakra and contemplating its essence, aspects, and functions can aid meditative concentration. When unbalanced life forces result in psychological and physical distress, one may be inclined to be confused, to wander aimlessly. When a soul is expressing through a physical body, its ability to function is determined by the actions of its life forces. Mental and physical health enable the soul to express more freely. It thus "rides upon" (its actions are supported by) its life force.

Kundalini, the "coiled" energy potential of the embodied soul, is confined at the base of the spine. It tends to remain dormant when attention is overly directed to externals (to personality- and body-centered awareness, ego-motivated purposes, excessive socialization, or compulsive need for sensory stimulation). The *brahmarandra* (aperture or opening at the crown of the head, the top of sushumna) is said to be closed when kundalini is dormant and opened when its energies move upward. When awakened kundalini energies (*shakti*) clarify soul awareness, the wisdom of Self-knowledge shines in the heart (true essence of being) of the accomplished kriya yoga practitioner.

The *sushumna* ("the radiant path") is referred to as "the path of God." When vital forces move upward through it, soul awareness is progressively unconfined or liberated. Soul force (primary prana) enters the body through the medulla oblongata at the base of the brain and flows downward to nourish the body and energize its functions. Kundalini is surplus, dormant soul force. From sushumna, the main channel, many channels are extended like branches of a tree. The life force flowing through the channel along the left side of sushumna is cooling and pacifying like the influence of the moon. The life force flowing through the right channel is heating and energizing, like the influence of the sun. Excessive "lunar" influence contributes to inertia (*tamas*); excessive "solar" influence is stimulating (*rajasic*).

Life force flows with greater dominance through the left or right channel for approximately two hours, then becomes dominant in the other channel for approximately two hours. When breathing is evenly balanced in both nostrils, the influence of life force in the sushumna is dominant, coherence of brain activity is likely, mental and emotional calmness prevails, awareness is more clear, and a sense of timelessness can be experienced.

Text:

Various influences of aspects of vital force move in all nadis. The five vital airs [pranas] go towards the skin, bones, and other places where they are influential.

Commentary:

The primary functional influences of the five aspects of prana are inhalation, exhalation and elimination of waste products, biochemical transformations, circulation, and upward movements of life forces.

Text:

Having acquired a thorough knowledge of the vital forces and their movements and functions, one should begin [yoga practice] with purification of the nadis. A devotee established in the moral and ethical observances, avoiding excessive company of others, having finished a course of study, delighting in truth and virtue, having conquered anger, being engaged in the service of the guru, and well-instructed in religious practices and the knowledge of one's station in life, should go to a sacred grove abounding in fruit, herbs, and water. A pleasant abode should be selected, frequented by knowers of God who persevere in the duties of their stations of life. Or in a temple, on the banks of a river or in a village or town, he should build a beautiful monastery. It should be clean and have every kind of protection. There, listening to the exposition of Vedanta, one should begin to practice yoga.

Having worshipped The Remover of All Obstacles, the devotee's preferred aspect of God should be reverently acknowledged. Sitting in a meditation posture on a soft seat, facing east or north, the learned devotee, keeping the head and neck erect and fixing the gaze at the spiritual eye, should see the sphere of the moon there and drink the flowing nectar.

Commentary:

Although the recommended, supportive conditions described

above are ideal for spiritual practice, it is not possible for everyone to have them. If one is prepared by prior study and is highly motivated, any quiet, wholesome and supportive environment will be suitable. Novice practitioners are advised to begin by cleansing the channels through which their vital forces flow. For this, pranayama practice is recommended. Prior to practice, one is advised to pray that all obstacles to success be removed and, with devotion, acknowledge one's preferred aspect of God.

Text:

Pranayama is said to be the union of prana and apana. It is of three kinds: inhalation, exhalation, and cessation of breathing. Om is said to be the basis of mantras to be used when practicing pranayama. Sitting in the chosen posture, one should meditate on Om. One should then draw in the air through the left nostril [holding the right nostril closed with a finger], momentarily pause, then exhale through the right nostril. The air is then drawn in through the right nostril. After a momentary pause, it is exhaled through the left nostril.

Commentary:

Prana is the primary aspect of life force instrumental during inhalation of air. Apana is the aspect of prana instrumental in exhalation of air and the removal of waste products from the body. Effective pranayama practice results in smooth flows of vital force, refined breathing, mental calmness, and clarity of awareness. Alternate nostril breathing is a basic pranayama routine. By its practice, air soon flows evenly through both nostrils, the prana-influences of the left and right channels are neutralized, and life force moves in the sushumna.

To improve concentration, a mantra can be used when this pranayama is practiced. One may mentally chant Om when inhaling and when exhaling. Any other mantra that might be used derives its power from Om (a contraction of AUM), the primordial, vibrating sound current that pervades the universe.

Text:

Then having become firm in the meditation posture, and preserving perfect self-control, to remove impurities from the sushumna the yogi should retain the inhaled air before exhaling it through the opposite nostril. One should practice cessation of the breath at sunrise, midday, sunset, and midnight for four weeks. In the early stages, perspiration is produced; in the middle stage there are tremors of the body; in the last stage the body levitates. When perspiration emerges, it should be massaged into the skin. By this means, the body becomes firm and light. There will be no burning sensation in the body as the result of practice. As with attentive care creatures are tamed, so also the breath, when rightly managed, is eventually regulated.

Commentary:

It is not convenient for the average person to practice at six-hour intervals each day. Two or three times a day can usually be scheduled. Breathing in through the left nostril and out through the right nostril, then in through the right nostril and out through the left nostril is one round. Ten to twenty rounds will be sufficient, starting with six to ten rounds and gradually increasing them without exerting effort. The retention of air after inhalation and the natural pause after exhalation is only momentary. There should be no attempt to forcibly hold the breath. Because this pranayama produces mental calmness, a good time to do it is when first sitting to meditate. If alternate nostril breathing is not used, kriya pranayama and the supplemental techniques will effectively cleanse (remove blockages from) the prana channels.

Text:

When the channels have been purified by regular practice of pranayama, life force easily moves upward through the sushumna. By contraction of the muscles of the neck and anal sphincter, vital force goes into sushumna. Drawing the vital force upward, the yogi, free from old age, becomes like a youth of sixteen. Breathing through both nostrils and drawing vital force upward, exhale through both nostrils. By this practice, hunger, thirst, lethargy, and sleepiness do not arise.

Commentary:

Mild contraction of the throat muscles and anal sphincter (the throat and root locks) may be practiced with mahamudra (or the alternative, supplemental technique) prior to kriya pranayama practice. During kriya pranayama practice, life force is drawn upward through the chakras into the brain with inhalation and is allowed to flow downward in reverse order with exhalation.

Text:

The restraint of breath and vital force is of two kinds: that which is accompanied by breathing; and that which is devoid of the actions of breathing. Until you have accomplished the isolation of stillness, practice pranayama. To one who has mastered breathlessness, nothing is unattainable. By it, knowledge of kundalini emerges; the body becomes lean, clear-eyed, and of serene countenance; vital forces flow upward; and the gastric fire [powers of digestion and assimilation] is increased.

Commentary:

After pranayama practice, breathing may be so subtle that it is barely noticeable. Between inhalation and exhalations, observe the intervals of nonbreathing. Notice that thoughts are either very subtle or nonexistent, sensory urges are weak or pacified, mundane desires are few or absent, and awareness is clear. The soul's urge to have its awareness fully restored to wholeness (the pure-conscious state) may then result in spontaneous kundalini awakening, effortless meditation, and enlivening and regeneration of the body.

Text:

Focusing attention on an inner object of contemplation is a secret [because little known] meditation technique. With mind and breath thus absorbed, one sees with the inner eye. This is *kechari* [being free in space] *mudra* [seal]. The seat [core essence] of nature is then revealed. With eyes partially closed and with firm concentration, fixing the gaze in the spiritual eye and becoming absorbed in the sun and moon, remaining firmly established in meditative contemplation, the yogi becomes aware of the light which transcends everything. Merging the sound in the light and elevating the brows a little results in mind-transcendence. Sabikalpa samadhi is then experienced. For one who accomplishes this, time does not exist.

Commentary:

When gazing into the spiritual eye during the tranquil state generated by kriya pranayama practice, focus attention on inner light and sound. If light is not perceived, continue to gaze steadily into the spiritual eye while listening to Om. The light of the spiritual eye is the reflected light of the medulla oblongata. When kundalini energies ascend through the chakras, the dual currents of life force flowing through the left and right channels beside the sushumna converge at the medulla center, hence the reference to absorption of attention in the "sun and moon." Elevating the brows helps to relax the muscles of the forehead and increases the pleasurable sensation at the spiritual eye. When attention is fully absorbed in the object of meditative contemplation, samadhi with the support of the meditative object is experienced. Then, with attention totally involved with the object of meditation, there is no awareness of external phenomena, including time.

Text:

Placing the awareness in the midst of shakti, and shakti in the midst of awareness, and looking inward, be happy. Place the Self in space and space in the Self. Having reduced everything to space, do not think of anything else. As salt in water becomes absorbed, so the devotee's awareness becomes absorbed in the true essence of what is contemplated.

Commentary:

The meditator's awareness and the life current flowing in the spine and brain blend when kriya pranayama is practiced with deep concentration. After pranayama practice, the meditator should dissolve awareness in space.

Text:

When knowledge of an object and the object cognized are both absent, that is the only path [for the meditator]. By giving up all cognition of objects, the mind is illumined. When the mind is illumined, awareness of Self [alone] remains.

Commentary:

Transcendent samadhi is an alert, unmodified superconscious state. Preliminary samadhi states may include a variety of moods and visual and auditory perceptions. Superconscious influences infused into the mind purify and illumine it.

Text:

For the dissolution of individualized awareness there are two ways: samadhi and knowledge. Samadhi is accomplished by restraining and pacifying the modifications and fluctuations of the mind. Knowledge is acquired by inquiry into the contents of the mind and other objects of knowledge. When modifications of the mind are quieted, mental peace results. When mental fluctuations cease, the cycles of births and deaths cease. When one does not yearn for mundane existence, or when desires have been satisfied, fluctuations of life force cease. Clarification of awareness may be accomplished by the study of scriptures, the company of good associates, indifference to sense pleasure, practice of yoga [the various procedures and superconsciousness], contemplation with alert attention focused on a desired object of concentration, or by firm adherence to living in accord with the laws of life.

By mastery of breath by practice of pranayama which does not cause fatigue, and by meditating in a secluded place, mental fluctuations cease. Through right realization of the true nature of the sound at the extreme end of the pronunciation of Om, and when dreamless sleep is rightly cognized, the fluctuations of prana cease. When consciousness is merged with life force that flows to the spiritual eye, the fluctuations of prana cease. When the spiritual eye becomes calm and clear so that the meditator can see into inner space, the fluctuations of prana cease. When thoughts and mental processes are dissolved into the spiritual eye, the fluctuations of prana cease. When knowledge which is beneficial and is untouched by any modifications is discerned as Om, only, and nothing else, the fluctuations of prana cease. By long contemplation on the fine essence of the heart, and by contemplation of the mind devoid of influential tendencies, fluctuations of prana cease. By these methods, and various others one may use, and by attunement with the consciousness of saints, fluctuations of prana cease.

Commentary:

Various practices can be used to still the random actions of the mind and life forces. Alternate nostril breathing can be practiced to quiet mental activities and relax the body. Attentive practice of kriya pranayama definitely stops fluctuations of the mind and vital forces. Note the recommendation to avoid tiredness when practicing and to meditate in a secluded place without distractions.

Contemplation and absorption of awareness in Om is a direct way to transcendence, as is insight into the dreamless sleep state. During dreamless sleep, mental processes are refined and the body's vital forces flow inward. By consciously duplicating the physiological characteristics of dreamless sleep, one can experience absolute, pure awareness.

By keeping attention and vital forces flowing into the spiritual eye when meditating, mental processes are refined and superconscious states are experienced. The "fine essence of the heart" to be contemplated is the true nature of the individualized Self in relationship to egoism (the illusional sense of independent existence) and its powers of intellectual discernment when in relationship to mind and matter.

When the devotee's thoughts and states of consciousness are attuned to those of the saints past and present of one's enlightenment tradition, the devotee's awareness is lifted out of self-conscious states into superconscious and transcendent states.

Text:

Having opened the door of kundalini by the practice of certain procedures, one should intentionally cause the door of liberation to be opened. Closing the door through which one's life forces should go, kundalini sleeps coiled like a serpent. The yogi who causes kundalini to move [and be freely expressive] is [soon] liberated. When kundalini is influential in the neck chakra [and higher], it contributes to liberation. In deluded people kundalini is influential in the lower regions of the body only. Leaving the two nadis [ida, the left channel in the spinal pathway, and pingala, the right channel], kundalini's shakti [vital energy] should move in the sushumna [the central pathway in the spine]. That channel is called "the path of God." To do this, one should practice pranayama [as directed by one's guru] with concentration. Practice should not be confined to daytime or night only, but should be scheduled to allow the most beneficial results as determined by the meditator's aspiration and commitment to practice.

When kechari mudra is practiced while sitting in meditation, the life forces which formerly flowed in the left and right channels of the spine are inclined to flow through sushumna. You should move the vital force through sushumna [by practicing kriya pranayama]. That is the location of kechari mudra. It is also located in the spiritual eye.

Commentary:

Kechari mudra is experienced when the meditator's awareness is no longer confined to physical or mental processes. A physical procedure also designated as kechari mudra, during which the tip of the tongue is made to touch the uvula for the purpose of directing flows of refined life forces to the brain, should be learned from one's teacher (if the teacher chooses to explain it) and not from anyone else or from books.

Text:

Firmly pressing the perineum with the left heel, drawing up the vital force to the neck and head chakras, stretching out the right leg, grasping the foot with both hands, momentarily retain the vital force in the higher centers. By this, prana is mastered and death is conquered. Then sit in meditation, contemplating your true Self in your field of awareness. In this way, direct perception [of the truth of being] is experienced.

Commentary:

This is *maha mudra*, practiced with the right leg extended, then with the left leg extended, then with both legs extended. Meditative contemplation on one's true nature and absolute Reality is advised. Death (unconsciousness) is overcome when the soul's vital forces are no longer restricted and awareness is no longer modified.

Text:

That one who retains the life force with concentrated attention at the spiritual eye, destroys all effects of past actions.

Commentary:

There can be no specific time-value placed on meditation practice and its results. When the meditator is established in transcendent realization for a sufficient duration of time, awareness may be permanently removed from self-conscious states and from the effects of conditions which may relate to those states.

Text:

By contemplating Om, all things [about God and processes of cosmic manifestation] are known. By transcending dharma and adharma, one knows the past and future. By contemplating the sound of creatures, knowledge of the causes of their utterances is obtained. By contemplating one's karma which is yet to be manifested, knowledge of previous incarnations spontaneously unfolds. By contemplating the mind of others, knowledge of their thoughts is obtained. By contemplating strength, one becomes strong. By contemplation on the sun [and solar system] knowledge of the sun and movements of the planets is obtained. By contemplation on the true Self, one obtains knowledge of the Spirit of God that nurtures the field of nature.

Commentary:

Some siddhis (powers of perfection) mentioned in chapter three of Patanjali's yoga-sutras are described. The ability to know the past and future is acquired when one's thoughts and actions, being knowledgeably spontaneous, are no longer restricted by thoughts about what is righteous (*dharma*) or what is unrighteous (*adharma*). When the devotee's awareness is removed from the mechanical laws of karma, relationships between causes and their effects may be intellectually and intuitively apprehended.

Text:

Internalization is withdrawing attention from the senses to avoid attachments to externals. Seeing everything that is observed as an expression of supreme Consciousness is such a practice, as is renunciation of attachments to the results of one's daily actions, withdrawing attention and directing it inward to meditate without distractions, and other procedures used to provide mastery of attention and of the senses.

Commentary:

Unless the ability to be soul-centered when engaged in ordinary activities and relationships is acquired, it is unlikely that one will be able to withdraw attention from externals (including the senses) and meditate effectively. Practice of superconscious meditation confers poise that enables one to relate to circumstances without becoming overly involved with them.

Text:

One can then successfully practice the three kinds of concentration: fixing attention on the true Self; contemplation on the inner space of the heart [being]; and contemplation on the five varieties of regulating influences of the five elements: earth, water, fire, air, and ether [space with cosmic forces].

Dhyana [meditation] naturally follows and is of two kinds: *saguna* [with the influences of the gunas or qualities of nature being present] and *nirguna* [without such influences]. The former is usually practiced with some form or aspect of God as the object of contemplation. The latter is contemplation on the reality of one's Self or on the Supreme Self.

Samadhi is the bringing together of awareness of the *jivatman* [individualized Self] and *Paramatman* [supreme Consciousness] without any sense of oneself as the knower, of that which is known as an object, or of knowledge. Its characteristics are supreme bliss [unqualified, joyous soul peace] and flawless realization of absolute or pure consciousness.

Commentary:

When *samadhi* (conscious oneness) is fully experienced, the meditator's awareness is not clouded or fragmented. There is no longer any sense of distinction between one's true Self and supreme Consciousness. Knowledge innate to the meditator's consciousness is self-revealed.

Text:

Then Shandilya, not [yet] having obtained [complete] knowledge of *Brahman* [the Absolute] described in the four Vedas [the texts of revealed knowledge], approached Atharvan and asked: "What is the knowledge of the Absolute? Teach me the way of knowing it by which I shall obtain that which is most excellent."

Atharvan:

The Absolute is *satya* [being-truth-reality]; knowledge, and the infinite Reality in which this world is interwoven; that from which all originated and into which all is absorbed; and which being known makes everything known. It is formless, unreachable [by the mind and intellect], and undefinable. It is to be cognized by [intuitive] knowledge and by yoga [samadhi]. It is that from which prana [life force] was projected. It is that which is nondual [one, without division]; which pervades everything like space; which is extremely subtle; without blemish; actionless; existence-being only; the essence of the bliss of consciousness; beneficent; calm; immortal; and beyond all phenomena. That is the absolute, pure field of Consciousness. You are That. Know That by joy and wisdom. That which is one; shining; the giver of the power of the true Self; the omniscient; the lord [that which regulates] of all and the inner reality of all beings; which abides in all beings; which is hidden in all beings and the source of all beings; which is realized only by yoga [samadhi] and creates, supports, and dissolves everything—that is the supreme Self. Comprehend the several [the many] worlds [realms] in the supreme Self. Do not grieve, O knower of the supreme Self; you shall attain the end of pain.

Commentary:

The reality of pure Consciousness can only be partially known by intellectual inquiry. One approach is to arrive at certainty of its existence by discarding all that it cannot be. It can be directly realized by practice of samadhi. Preliminary samadhi states (*sabikalpa*, with support) provide experience and knowledge of various aspects of the mind and of nature. Transcendent samadhi (*nirbikalpa*, without the support of mental actions or of perceptions of nature's forces) is full knowledge of supreme Consciousness. The teacher says, "I can tell you about it, but you will have to know it by direct realization." Shandilya is told, "You are That (supreme Consciousness)." When it is realized, delusions and illusions, the causes of confusion and suffering, vanish.

Shandilya:

From supreme Consciousness, the source of Om, imperishable, actionless, beneficial, and pure existence only, how does this universe arise? How does it exist in supreme Consciousness? How is it absorbed in it? Please solve these mysteries for me.

Atharvan:

Supreme Consciousness is imperishable and actionless. From its formlessness, three forms [aspects] arise: that which is without characteristics; that which has characteristics; and that which is with and without characteristics. That which is pure reality, consciousness, and bliss of Self-awareness, without modifications, omnipresent, and most subtle, undefinable and eternal, is the formless aspect. *Mahesvara* [*maha*, great; *Ishwara*, lord or ruling influence] with *maya* [primordial nature] or *avidya* [not-knowledge] is the aspect with and without characteristics. An impulse within God resulted in the bringing forth of universal manifestation. That aspect of Consciousness endowed with all resources, which is all-pervading and established in the hearts of all beings, the regulating influence which manifests primordial nature, is God. In God's omnipresent consciousness are all of the gods [aspects of ruling forces] and beings [individualized souls]. The aspect which regulates the creative force of Consciousness is kind to devotees, untouched by anything, and has characteristics [of transformative influences] only.

Commentary:

The first manifesting aspect of Consciousness with discernible characteristics is the Godhead, the Oversoul with potential to impel the processes of manifestation. The intelligence aspect that rules or regulates primordial nature is without characteristics; its qualities (gunas) are its causative, expressive characteristics. The aspect with characteristics which controls cosmic forces and is supportive of devotees while remaining untouched by anything in nature has qualities which make possible its transformative, redemptive actions. Primordial nature is said to be without knowledge of its own because its actions are directed by intelligence innate to Om, its cause.

In Vedic scriptures, the expanding, manifesting aspect of God is named *Brahma*. The aspect which sustains (preserves) creation is named *Vishnu*. The aspect which participates in change and transformation is named *Shiva* and is revered by yogis intent upon inner transformation that allows unfoldment of Self-knowledge and liberation of consciousness. Although Brahma, Vishnu, and Shiva are often depicted as personalized beings, they are but expressive aspects of God. Likewise, the gods and goddesses referred to in Vedic scriptures are God's various powers and qualities. Devotees may personalize them in an endeavor to establish a sympathetic relationship and invite their beneficial influences.

Text:

That which is alone Real and is the essence of the bliss of Consciousness—why is it referred to as the transcendent supreme Consciousness? Because it expands and causes everything to expand. Why is it referred to as the indwelling Self? Because it contains everything, absorbs everything, and is everything. Why is it called the Great Lord? Because by its own power it governs all things. One who knows these secret [subtle] meanings knows everything. That devotee who contemplates supreme Consciousness as one's Self becomes a knower of supreme Consciousness. That devotee who always contemplates [and comprehends] the reality of God in relationship to nature is freed from all errors and awakens to full realization of the Absolute.

Commentary:

When the Self relates to a mind and body and assumes a viewpoint of being a mind or body, it is referred to as a soul. This error in perception does not change the fact that the Self is ever what it is: pure Consciousness-Existence. To be Self-realized is to be fully awake to our true nature.

Thus Ends This Upanishad.

CHAPTER SIX

The Inner Meaning of the Bhagavad Gita

The Bhagavad Gita has spiritually nurtured and inspired millions of readers for over two thousand years. The common translation of the title is descriptive of a holy or divine song: *bhaj*, reverence or love, to share wealth and glory; and *gita*, from the verb-root *gai*, to sing. The prefix *srimad* (or *shrimat*), from the verb-root *sri*, to flame, to spread or pour out light, is usually used in the title.

The two central characters in the story are Arjuna and Krishna. Arjuna represents the seeker of knowledge and experience of God. Krishna, Arjuna's cousin, friend, teacher, and the personification of divine power and grace in human form, represents the indwelling Spirit of God. In eighteen chapters, a broad range of philosophical views are explored and practical instruction about how to live skillfully and fulfill personal destiny is expounded. The inner message of the Gita explains how to awaken to Self-knowledge and God-realization. Although many devotees presume the text to affirm God to be a cosmic person whose name is Krishna, insightful analysis reveals that what is indicated is a transcendent Reality which, formless and nameless, is beyond all categories, therefore, indescribable although realizable.

Facts about the historical Krishna are minimal. Several "Krishnas" are mentioned in various texts written over a period of several hundred years, starting perhaps as early as 800 B.C.E., and two distinct story-traditions can be discerned. 1) A Vasudeva-Krishna, a warrior-prince who helps the Pandava brothers in a war against their cousins, is portrayed as an incarnation of the qualities of the aspect of God which restores and preserves the cosmic order and teaches a syncretistic (reconciliation of various beliefs) path of devotion and yoga practice. 2) A cowherd (*Gopala*) Krishna who as a child is mischievous, plays a flute to attract and innocently flirt with the young cowherd girls (*gopis*), and eventually chooses one of them (*Radha*) to be his wife. Most of the stories are symbolic and describe a variety of interactions between the Spirit of God and the field of nature.

In the epic *Mahabharata* ("great story of the descendents of Bharata") of which the Bhagavad Gita is a part, Krishna is described by the author *Vyasa* (the "arranger" who assembles and presents information) as an avatar, an embodiment of divine qualities who appears on the scene whenever needed to restore virtue to the world. His words represent the soul's wisdom that is being Self-revealed to Arjuna.

When read superficially, the Bhagavad Gita tells of a great war that occurred between opposing factions, who were cousins, on a battlefield north of the present-day city of New Delhi, India. As an allegory—a story in which characters, objects, and events symbolically illustrate ideas or moral and spiritual principles—the esoteric meaning portrays a drama far more significant than a transitory historical event. The insightful reader is provided with the following information: (1) the progress of the soul's awakening from self-conscious involvements with physical and psychological circumstances to realization of its true nature as pure consciousness; (2) the challenges commonly confronted during the process; (3) liberating knowledge which removes awareness from all that is suppressive and restrictive.

The truths explained in the Bhagavad Gita have great value to every person who sincerely aspires to an understanding of life's processes and of ways to facilitate rapid, authentic spiritual growth that culminates in illumination of consciousness and soul liberation. Ordinary illusional, sense-bound human existence is often painful and may seem to be devoid of meaningful purpose. What is needed is for the mind to be illumined by the soul's innate light and for the senses to be subject to the soul's capacity to freely choose. Self-consciousness is then transcended and life flows smoothly under the direction of soul-originated impulses referred to as grace. The actions of grace are the effective influences of the inclination of the Spirit of God indwelling nature to fulfill the purposes of life.

As soul-mind-body beings relating to the physical realm, we are instinctively and intuitively directed to fulfill basic desires and to satisfy needs essential to our survival, security, well-being, and continued growth. To this end, we innately want to live in harmony with nature's processes, have life-enhancing desires easily fulfilled, experience spontaneous satisfaction of needs, and know of and unfold our spiritual potential. When soul awareness is not yet pronounced, we may be inclined to direct most of our attention to satisfying our physical and emotional needs while ignoring or neglecting our spiritual growth. Although such behavior may result in marginal human happiness, it will not satisfy the deep-seated desire of the heart (real essence of being) to awaken to Self-knowledge which allows God-experience and transcendent realizations.

In Sanskrit literature, the first chapter serves as the introduction to the main body of the text. To have access to the core message, we have to carefully examine this chapter to acquire an understanding of the author's purpose for writing the Bhagavad Gita and learn the esoteric meanings of the names of the main characters of the story. In the lengthy Mahabharata epic, of which the Gita is but a small part, tradition and folklore are interwoven with symbolism in narrating the history of Bharata, an ancient King, and his descendents. The main characters of the drama are introduced in the following unusual ways:

In ancient India, at Hastinapur, there lived a king of the solar dynasty whose name was Santanu. The first of his two queens was named Ganga. When she deserted him under unusual circumstances, he wed Satyavati.

Walking beside the Ganges River, King Santanu met Ganga and asked her to be his wife. He did not then know that she was actually a manifestation of the river in human form. Ganga agreed to his proposal only after the King promised not to interfere with anything she might do after they married. If he ever questioned her actions, she declared, she would forsake him immediately.

When their first son was born, Ganga carried the infant from the palace and threw it into the river. The King, although much disturbed by her behavior, because of his prior promise not to interfere did not attempt to prevent it.

Six more sons were born, and each of them was given to the Ganges by the Queen. When the eighth son was born, the King implored her not to do with that infant as she had done with the first seven. True to her word, Ganga left her husband and her eighth son. Rushing to the Ganges River, she threw herself into it and merged in the waters.

King Santanu lavished affection upon his remaining son, Devavrata, providing for his education and training in all the arts and skills befitting a prince and heir.

One day, the King went hunting in the forest. Resting under the shade of a tree by a river, he saw lotus petals floating on the waters. Following the stream of petals to their source, he saw a charming damsel, Satyavati, putting them into the river as a ritual offering.

Remaining out of the young woman's sight, the King followed her when she returned home, where she lived with her father, Dasa Raja, known as the fisher-king because his main activity was fishing. Santanu talked with Dasa Raja, requesting consent for Satyavati to be his wife.

Dasa Raja agreed, insisting, however, that his daughter be the principal wife and that her first son be the successor to the throne.

King Santanu refused the terms of marriage and returned to his palace. As time passed, everyone around him became aware of his unhappiness. Prince Devavrata decided to do something about the situation. Without telling anyone of his plan, he went alone to Dasa Raja and asked him to consent to the marriage of Satyavati and his father. To reassure Dasa Raja about his daughter's future and that of any future sons, Prince Devavrata promised that he would not himself claim the throne and that he would never marry or have any children. Because of these two awesome vows, Prince Devavrata thereafter became known as Bhishma (the formidable).

King Santanu and Satyavati were married. Two sons were born: Chitrangada, who died at an early age, and Vichitravirya, who was peculiar and weak. After Santanu's demise, Vichitravirya became King, but because he was weak the kingdom was really ruled by Bhishma.

Bhishma decided that when Vichitravirya grew to adulthood he should have a queen. With this plan in mind, he went to the court of the King of Kashi where a gathering of royal families assembled for the purpose of having their daughters choose husbands from among the princes who were invited to be there. The King of Kashi had three marriageable daughters. In keeping with the tradition of the time and culture—of sometimes kidnapping women for the purpose of marriage—Bhishma waited until the three daughters wandered away from the larger group, put them into his chariot, and rushed toward Hastinapur.

The names of the women were Amba, Ambika, and Ambalika. Amba prayed to be released because, in her heart, she had already promised herself to another. Bhishma let her go and continued his journey with the two remaining sisters.

King Vichitravirya, because of his weak constitution, died soon after marrying Ambika and Ambalika. His two widowed wives were then introduced to the sage Veda Vyasa, and by him each had a son. Ambika's son, Dhritarashtra, was born blind. Ambalika's son, Pandu, was of light complexion. Bhishma continued to rule the kingdom. When the sons grew to adulthood, Pandu was put on the throne because Dhritarashtra, his older half brother who would have otherwise ruled, was blind.

Pandu had two wives, Kunti and Madri. Before her marriage, Kunti, testing the power of a mantra she had learned from a sage, inadvertently invoked the blessings of the sun and gave birth to a male child. Because it was considered to be illegitimate, the child was adopted by a carpenter and later became known as Karna, a hero of the Kaurava clan. After her marriage, Kunti invoked the gods (divine forces) which controlled dharma (righteous actions), prana (vital forces), and Indra (god of fire, the power of transformation). Thus were born Yudhisthira, Bhima, and Arjuna. Kunti then taught the mantra to Madri, who could only use it once. Madri's invocation of two gods produced twin sons, Nakul and Sahadeva. Because they were considered to be the progeny of Pandu, the five sons were known as the Pandavas.

When the five brothers grew to adulthood, they participated in a contest arranged by King Drupada for the purpose of having a husband chosen for his daughter, Draupadi. Participants in the contest had to lift a heavy bow, string it, and shoot an arrow through the eye of a fish that was hanging above a revolving wheel with a hole in the center. More, they had to aim at the target by looking into a reflecting pool beneath it. Arjuna, among all of the contestants, was successful. Returning to their home with Draupadi, the brothers asked Kunti, their mother, to come out of the house. She replied, "Whatever you have brought, share among yourselves." Draupadi thus became the wife of the five Pandava brothers.

The blind Dhritarashtra, half brother to King Pandu, fathered one hundred sons and one daughter, cousins of the five Pandava brothers. When King Pandu died, Duryodhana, the firstborn son of Dhritarashtra, sought the throne which he felt was rightfully his because his blind father had been denied it. When Yudhisthira, the eldest Pandava, was put on the throne instead, Duryodhana conspired to remove him from rulership of the kingdom. To do this, advised by a conspirator to use loaded dice, he challenged Yudhisthira to a dice game. It was agreed that whoever should lose would go into exile for twelve years, then retire into seclusion for one year. Yudhisthira lost the game, and with his four brothers and their wife, Draupadi, departed for the agreed upon period of time. Duryodhana assumed rulership of the kingdom.

After thirteen years, the brothers returned to Hastinapur to reclaim their rights, but were refused them. Civil war was declared. All of the royal families of that region of India took sides and gathered their armies. Krishna, a king, and cousin of the Pandavas, asked the opposing factions to choose either him or his army. He would not participate in the battle, but would put his army at the disposal of whoever wanted it, while remaining with the other side.

What are we to think about this amazing story? We learn of a King who weds an embodiment of the Ganges River who, for reasons of her own, throws her first seven sons into the river and merges into it when she is not allowed to dispatch her eighth son as she did the first seven. We learn of plural marriages, children conceived by the power of mantra, manipulative behaviors, intrigue, deception, and finally, a decision to engage in battle. What can we learn from it? The key to understanding the drama is to discover what the names of the characters mean and what their actions and experiences reveal. To do this, we have to examine the mythical genealogy and the unique behaviors of the participants according to the concepts of the philosophical system known as Samkhya—the numbering and classification of the categories of the emanations and manifestations of Consciousness.

Santanu, (pure Consciousness) interacted with Ganga (the intelligence of Om). Eight aspects of Consciousness were produced: seven remain subjective; the eighth is objective.

The seven hidden aspects which regulate subjective cosmic processes are: two aspects, cosmic and individualized, at the level of causal or fine cosmic forces of creation; two aspects, cosmic and individualized, at the level of astral or subtle life forces; two aspects, cosmic and individualized, at the level of gross physical creation; and one all-pervading aspect. Although in some religious traditions these are referred to as gods, they represent various aspects, influences, and powers of Consciousness.

In Vedic texts, the two aspects at the causal level are referred to as Vishnu, that which preserves or maintains. The two aspects at the astral level are referred to as Brahma, that which expands and is the cause of manifestation. The two aspects at the physical level are referred to as Shiva, that which causes change and transformation; also Maheshvara, the "great lord" or ruler. The seventh, hidden aspect, is the Spirit of God pervading the cosmos without itself being confined to or limited by it.

The eighth aspect, which does not remain hidden, is cosmic individuality: Bhishma, the witness aspect of Consciousness which participates in outer affairs but is not itself the determining factor. Because it is unmarried (aloof from creation), it does not produce anything. It and the Spirit of God are like two faces of Consciousness: the former looks outward into the realm of objective nature, the latter remains subjective. The Sanskrit word for the all-pervading Spirit, the consciousness of God aspect, is *Kutastha Chaitanya*, "the one on the summit." It is referred to by some Hindu devotees as Krishna Consciousness. Also, some devotees personalize it in order to feel that they have a close relationship with it.

Interacting with the unconscious aspect of primordial nature (Satyavati, that which embodies *sat*, the truth of being) the Spirit of God (the enlivening aspect of Consciousness) causes the field of primordial nature (Om and its aspects of space, time, and cosmic forces) to undergo changes which produce outward manifestations of itself. The first to manifest (the first child of Satyavati) is the aspect of the field of primordial nature undergoing mutation from fine to gross expression which does not last long (Chitrangada). Satyavati's second son, Vichitravirya (the illusional sense of independent existence, ego consciousness) which, although peculiar (distinctly different) and weak, is necessary for the processes of creation to occur. Because it is contractive and illusional, it is ultimately powerless. It conceals knowledge but is not possessed of knowledge.

The two wives of ego consciousness (Vichitravirya) are doubt (Ambika) and the power of discrimination (Ambalika). The other sister, Amba, chose not to marry because she was promised to another (involved with sensation through the lower chakras). In the story, Vichitravirya died soon after marrying his wives. It was then arranged for them to have children by the sage Veda Vyasa (wisdom-knowledge). From knowledge and doubt (Ambika), blind mind (Dhritarashtra) is born. From knowledge and discrimination (Ambalika) pure intelligence (Pandu) is born.

Dhritarashtra and his wives had one hundred sons and one daughter. Blind or deluded mind influenced by sentiment or feeling produced numberless self-serving tendencies. The first of these was Duryodhana (passion, lower desire that is difficult to overcome and causes many problems). Although both Dhritarashtra and Pandu belonged to the Kuru clan, only Dhritarashtra was known as its chief representative because, with Bhishma's help, he ruled the kingdom.

Pandu (pure intelligence) with his two wives: Kunti (kundalini's power of attraction, dispassionate compassion, and discernment which banishes error), and Madri (intellect influenced by sentiment) secluded himself in the forest. He was, therefore, away from the kingdom (of the mind). Yogis teach the front part of the body to be the realm of mental and physical impulses and tendencies. The back, the spinal pathway, rules spiritual inclinations. Dhritarashtra's children are referred to as Kauravas (representative of self-serving, destructive or trouble-causing tendencies and habits rooted in the mind) which are considered to be enemies of the soul's aspiration to be enlightened. Pure intelligence, like Pandu in the story, remains aloof; the mind, like Dhritarashtra, rules material affairs.

By the power of mantra, the two wives of Pandu produced five sons, referred to as the Pandavas (the products of pure intelligence). Kunti (kundalini's power of attraction, dispassionate compassion, and discernment which banishes error) produced three sons, Yudhisthira, Bhima, and Arjuna—symbolic of the essences (*tattvas*) of the subtle elements of the three higher chakras in the spinal pathway.

Yudhisthira (righteousness, dharma, steadfast and firm) is the ether element essence of the throat chakra at the cervical region of the spine.

Bhima (dauntlessness, pranayama, control of vital forces, endless strength, formidable) is the air element essence of the heart chakra at the dorsal region of the spine.

Arjuna (purity of mind and heart, the aspiration to excellence, fiery self-control) is the fire element essence of the lumbar chakra, midway between the higher and lower chakras.

Pandu's second wife, Madri (spiritual intellect influenced by sentiment), gave birth to twins which symbolize the element influences of the two lower chakras.

Nakula (the stillness of the mind, the power to adhere) is the water element essence of the chakra at the sacral region of the spine.

Sahadeva (the power of resistance) is the earth element-essence of the chakra at the base of the spine.

Draupadi, the wife of the five Pandava brothers, represents kundalini shakti: the flowing, harmonizing, enlivening actions of the creative power of the soul expressive in the body. The five sons of Draupadi are the sound and light frequencies perceived in the chakras when they are enlivened by kundalini energies.

The eldest Pandava brother, Yudhisthira (righteousness) the fifth chakra state of consciousness, gambled with his eldest cousin, Duryodhana (egotism, lower desire, jealousy, pride), lost the game, and was banished. When righteousness plays with unrighteousness, when soul awareness interacts with conditioned mental tendencies and sense attractions, errors in judgment can occur, causing clouding of awareness. To reclaim the former status, one must withdraw for a period of time to become grounded in the virtues and engage in spiritual practices to be empowered to again confront that which restricts the soul's freedom of expression and the fulfillment of its destiny. Hence, the symbolism of the Pandavas having to be exiled, going into seclusion, and returning to engage in battle.

When Krishna (enlightened consciousness) offered his services to one of the opposing factions and his army to the other, the Kauravas (the self-serving mental tendencies) chose the army. The Pandavas chose Krishna, who agreed to drive Arjuna's chariot. The outcome of the forthcoming contest was then already decided, for where there is Krishna (enlightened consciousness), victory is certain. In the Bhagavad Gita story, Arjuna's chariot is the body with the five senses (horses) driven (governed) by enlightened consciousness.

Translating and commenting on the Bhagavad Gita requires careful attention to details. Some scholars believe that through the years minor changes and additions may have been made in the text. The Mahabharata, which includes the eighteen chapters of the Gita, was for many centuries memorized and communicated by storytellers. The elaborate, colorful, and often dramatic narrative made it easier to remember and popular with people in all walks of life. Even without knowledge of its inner meaning, listeners (and, later, readers) could derive benefit at whatever level the story was comprehended.

At an exoteric level, there is much of value to be learned in regard to meaningful human existence, the well-being of society, and the importance and usefulness of sustained spiritual aspiration. The esoteric message has value to those who are perceptive enough to understand it. Because the concepts set forth were already well-known when it was composed, the information is considered to be traditional or remembered knowledge rather than a new revelation. It is, however, accepted as an authentic scripture of yoga.

The story begins as a great war between rival factions is about to begin. The incidents described and the dialogue provided for the symbolic characters portray the drama of individual psychological transformation and spiritual growth. The words attributed to Arjuna and Krishna, and of the few other characters who are given lines to speak, were written for the purpose of describing timeless truths.

Dhritarashtra represents unenlightened mind, the father of the material aspects of nature and ruler of the kingdom of the senses. Knowledge of transformative processes cannot be apprehended by a mind governed by partial understanding devoid of discernment. In the story, Dhritarashtra, blind and residing at a place distant from where the armies are gathered, relies on his counselor, Sanjaya, to report on what is transpiring. Sanjaya, with powers of clairvoyance which enable him to see with inner vision, represents every person's faculty of impartial intuitive perception that, when called upon during occasions of introspection, provides insight. The story begins with Dhritarashtra's question:

> Assembled on dharmakshetra-kurukshetra, desirous to fight,
> what did my sons and the sons of Pandu do, Sanjaya?

Dharma is righteousness, virtue, morality: that which upholds or supports evolution's inclination toward transformation, growth, and expression. The impulses of Consciousness which enhance life are dharmic. Kshetra is the field (place) where actions occur. The word kuru is used to refer to the characteristics and tendencies of the deluded mind. This first verse sets the stage for the drama which is to take place in the field where righteousness confronts unrighteousness. Where is this field? Since the story describes the soul's restoration of its awareness to wholeness, the place where righteousness must overcome unrighteousness is the devotee's individualized awareness.

Arjuna's questions and comments testify to the soul's aspiration to awaken to Self-knowledge and realization of God, and of its conflicts, struggles, and endeavors to learn what is true and how to actualize it. In the story, Arjuna is portrayed as a warrior who must fulfill his duty in a responsible manner. He represents the soul at a critical stage of spiritual growth, still somewhat grounded in physical and mental awareness (third chakra characteristics), yet beginning to awaken to higher understanding. The progression of unfoldment is from confusion to the fourth chakra devotee stage devoid of ego-fixation; the fifth chakra stage of apprehension of higher realities; the sixth chakra stage of revelation; to final unfoldment of innate knowledge that culminates in illumination of consciousness.

PART THREE

*Meditation Techniques and Routines
for All Levels of Practice*

*Answers to Questions
About the Spiritual Path*

CHAPTER SEVEN

Meditation Techniques and Routines for All Levels of Practice

A meditation technique is only a "tool" to use until it is not needed. The routines described in this chapter can be adapted to your personal needs and capacity to practice.

For best results, meditate daily on a regular schedule. An ideal time to meditate is early in the morning when your mind and emotions are calm after a night of restful sleep. If you prefer to meditate later in the day, do it at the same time every day to establish the habit of meditating.

Your meditation environment should be clean and quiet. It can be helpful to have a special place to practice; a room or a nook in a room where you can be alone. Having a small alter or other devotional items and your favorite spiritual literature there is optional.

Turn telephones off so you won't be disturbed.

If you pray quietly, or silently, to invoke divine assistance, do it at the beginning of your practice session.

If you are a novice meditator, begin with the first routine. Use the other routines as your proficiency improves and as you feel inclined to do so. You will learn to meditate skillfully by your regular, attentive, patient practice.

Remember that the purpose of your practice is to become mentally and emotionally calm and have your consciousness clarified—restored to wholeness.

Meditate each day more deeply than you did the day before.
— *Paramahansa Yogananda*

1. Meditation Practice For Everyone

This routine is recommended for beginning meditators and for experienced meditators who need to be reminded of the basic procedure. Practice time: 20 to 30 minutes.

• Sit upright, poised and alert, with your attention directed to the front and higher regions of your brain.
• If you pray to invoke divine assistance, do it now.
• If meditation flows spontaneously, let your innate urge to be spiritually awake determine your experience.
• If meditation does not flow spontaneously, use a mantra: a word or word-phrase to focus your attention.
• When your mind is calm and your attention is focused, disregard the mantra and rest in the peaceful silence for as long as you feel inclined to do so.
• Conclude your practice session. Maintain your calm state of mind and awareness after meditation.

How to Use a Mantra

If you already have a mantra that is pleasant to use, use it. If you do not have a mantra, for a one word mantra, use "Om," "God," "peace," or any word that pleases you. A two-syllable mantra can be "Om–God," "Om–peace" or any word-phrase of your choice. Traditional two-syllable Sanskrit mantras that some meditators enjoy using are "so–ham" or hong–sau."

When using a one-word mantra: feel air flowing into your nose when you breathe in; mentally speak the mantra as you exhale and feel peaceful.

When using a two-word mantra or word-phrase: mentally speak the first word when you inhale and mentally speak the second word when you exhale.

I absorbed my attention within and realized my true Self.
– Kabir

2. Light and Sound Contemplation

When your mind is calm and your attention is internalized, look into the spiritual eye and be aware in the higher brain.

- If you see a light, let your attention be attracted to it and let your awareness merge with it. The appearance of inner light is not a supernatural event; it may be seen when your mind is calm, when brain centers are stimulated by your concentration, or when your life force flows upward into the brain.
- Listen in your ears or in the space around your head. When a sound-frequency is heard, gently try to hear a subtle sound behind it. Continue in this way until the sound that is heard flows in a steady stream. Consider that sound to be the vibration of Om. Merge your attention and awareness in the sound and let your consciousness expand.

If light and sound are perceived simultaneously, merge your attention and awareness in light and sound. If you do not see inner light, concentrate on the sound current.

Let your devotion to God be like a wood fire that burns
steadily for a long time; not like a straw fire that produces
a bright flame then quickly goes out.
— *Paramahansa Yogananda*

3. Moving Awareness Through The Chakras

This is a supplemental technique to use after sitting for a while and you want to refresh your practice and improve your concentration.

- Look into the spiritual eye while being aware of your spine. *Feel it.* Mentally picture the chakras, starting at the bottom and going upwards through the spine into the spiritual eye and higher brain.
- Starting at the base chakra, feel it, mentally chant Om once. Feel and imagine the sound of Om to be emanating from that chakra. Locate the second chakra and mentally chant Om once while feeling that the sound is emanating from it. Continue in this way to the third, fourth, and fifth chakras, the spiritual eye, and crown chakra.
- Pause for a moment, then go down through the chakras to the base chakra, chanting Om once at each chakra and feeling the vibration response.
- Pause for a moment, then repeat the procedure.
- Do this a few times, concluding the practice of this technique at the crown chakra. Listen to Om and merge with it.

I was long enslaved by the great enemy, ignorance, which robbed me of my wealth of wisdom. But now, by God's grace and my own excellent self-endeavor, I have attained wisdom. By Self-knowledge the shadow of ego-sense has been removed. Rid of the poverty of delusion, I remain supremely free. All that is worth knowing is now known. All that is worth seeking has been seen. I have attained *that* beyond which there is nothing to be attained. – *Vashishta's Yoga*

4. Cultivating Cosmic Consciousness

You can use this technique to expand your consciousness.

- Look into the spiritual eye and visualize a blue ball of light of any size and any shade of blue of your choosing.
- Identify with it. Imagine that you are conscious, blue light.
- As conscious, blue light, expand until you fill your head.
- Expand until you fill your body, then extend beyond the boundaries of your body.
- Expand until you fill the room in which you are sitting.
- Expand beyond the building in which you abide (or the local environment if you are sitting outside).
- Swiftly expand until you fill the planet, then "see" and feel that Planet Earth is floating within your consciousness.
- Expand until our solar system is floating within you, then expand until the Milky Way Galaxy is floating within you.
- Expand until all of the billions of galaxies in our universe are floating in your consciousness.
- Knowing the field of primordial nature (Om and its attributes of space, time, and fine cosmic forces) to be the field from which our universe emanates, contemplate it and identify with it (using your imagination).
- Contemplate the Oversoul, source of Om. Identify with it.
- Contemplate pure, existence-being.
- Serenely abide for a while in the silence.

Few people whose awareness is ordinary know that
the reality of God extends fully to this earth realm.
— *Mahavatar Babaji, guru of Lahiri Mahasaya*

Guidelines For Kriya Initiates

If you have been initiated into the meditation practices of the kriya yoga tradition that I represent or by another teacher in this tradition, practice as you were instructed.

Here are some guidelines:

- Meditate on a regular schedule.
- After practicing a technique, rest in the silence for a while with your attention and awareness in the higher brain.
- Stay alert and attentive.
- Avoid impatience. Aspire to be fully, spiritually awake and let your innate knowledge of your true nature emerge.
- Balance your meditation practices with attentive, effective living. Avoid becoming introverted or disinterested in duties and meaningful relationships.
- Avoid superficial or excessive metaphysical discussions with others. Concentrate on your spiritual practices and duties. Endeavor to live a Self- and God-centered life: avoid talking about it or dramatizing your devotion.
- Nurture mental and spiritual attunement with the lineage of gurus of this kriya yoga tradition.

If you are an initiate of a different enlightenment tradition, adhere to the practices of that path.

If you are a devout adherent of a traditional religious faith, practice the modes of worship that are meaningful to you and practice meditation for the psychological and physiological benefits and to quicken your spiritual growth.

When the wavelike changes in mind and awareness are transcended by concentrated meditation, our purified consciousness is one with supreme Consciousness. – *Lahiri Mahasaya, guru of Sri Yukteswar*

Alternative Ways to Conclude Your Meditation Practice

You may end your practice session by opening your eyes and sitting for a few moments to enjoy the peaceful silence and your sense of well-being.

Or you may come out of meditation gradually. Feel free to experiment until you discover the way that is most helpful to you. The following routine is only an example.

- Be peaceful. Feel comfortable in the universe. Know that as you live effectively and appropriately in accord with your highest understanding, you have the full support of the forces of nature and of God's grace.
- Know and feel that the necessary resources and supportive events, circumstances, and personal relationships that are for your highest good are easily provided. Feel thankful.
- Acknowledge all souls in the universe, including the subtle realms. Wish for their highest good. See them in God. See them spiritually enlightened. See them fulfilled and happy.
- Abide in this awareness of wholeness for a few minutes, then conclude your practice session.

Your clear state of consciousness keeps you attuned with the Infinite and blends with the collective consciousness of all souls everywhere to bless them and enhance their lives.

Affirmation

The enlivening reality of God is freely expressive in and through me. It illumines my mind, regenerates my body, removes all restrictions to its flow, inspires me with creative ideas, empowers my constructive actions, and harmoniously arranges all of my circumstances and relationships in divine order.

Supportive Lifestyle Routines

Wholesome, intentional, right living is beneficial spiritual practice. Well-ordered lifestyle routines contribute to health, mental peace, and total well-being.

Adopt the these recommended routines in ways that are compatible with your personal circumstances.

- Schedule your activities and duties to provide a balance of activity, rest, and recreation.
- Obtain sufficient sleep to refresh your mind and body.
- Start each day with thoughts of God and your relationship with God. Pray and meditate.
- Perform all duties and other actions skillfully. Be attentive and alert.
- Decide how much time to devote to work, social interaction, personal or family duties, community service, metaphysical studies, and meditation practice.
- Exercise on a regular schedule. Walk, swim, play tennis or golf, ride a bicycle, use weights to strengthen your muscles and maintain bone density, practice hatha yoga or tai chi. Choose exercise that is best suited to your needs and your basic mind-body constitution.
- Choose a low-calorie, nutrition-rich diet of natural foods.
- Manage stress by nurturing peace of mind, avoiding worry and anxiety, and daily meditation.
- Cultivate the virtues and constructive practices described in chapter two, sutras 30 and 32.
- Nurture optimism and joyfulness. Be happy.

> To understand what our real needs are, we should
> rely on observation, experimentation, and reason.
> *— Swami Sri Yukteswar, guru of Paramahansa Yogananda*

> Life has to be lived. Why not live it in the highest way?
> *— Paramahansa Yogananda*

CHAPTER EIGHT

Answers to Questions
About The Spiritual Path

These questions are commonly asked by individuals who aspire to Self- and God-realization.

Is it possible for me to be Self-realized in my current lifetime?

Yes. Aspire to be fully, spiritually awake, concentrate on essential matters; minimize or disregard what is not essential. Live effectively, study to acquire higher knowledge, and practice meditation on a regular schedule until you are proficient in eliciting superconscious states. Remember the importance of seeing through, and rising above, the illusion that you are other than a spiritual being. Persist with unwavering faith.

During my first private talk with my guru, he advised me about lifestyle regimens, study, and meditation practice, then said, "Read a little; meditate more; think of God all the time."

A little over two years later, during our last private time together a few weeks before he left this world, he said, "Don't be overly concerned about what others do or don't do. Don't look back. Don't look to the left or to the right. Look straight ahead to the goal [of Self- and God-realization] and go all the way in this lifetime. You can do it."

Self-realization: How influential are my personal endeavors? How influential is karma? Is it possible to be influenced by another person's karma? How influential is grace?

Your right personal endeavors will calm and purify your mind, clarify your awareness, allow your divine qualities to emerge, and unveil your innate knowledge of what you are in relationship to the wholeness of life.

As your Self-knowing improves, all troublesome karmic influences will be weakened and neutralized. Avoid thinking that you have karma. Karmic conditions are mental traces of prior thoughts, feelings, desires, and memories. As a spiritual being you are superior to your mind and its contents. If you have a strong subconscious drive to be spiritually awake, nurture it until your aspiration replaces it.

You can be influenced by the mental and emotional states and states of consciousness of others if you react to their words, moods, or behaviors, just as they can be influenced by what you say, how you feel, and what you do. Allow only constructive influences to prevail in your life and help others with your positive words and actions.

As you become receptive and responsive, the supportive impulses of life will be expressive within and around you.

Is a guru-disciple relationship suitable for truth seekers in the West who have a pronounced sense of individualism?

Individualism is a desire or inclination to assert one's will and personality; to succeed by one's own initiative.

Truth seekers should have the will and the functional abilities to accomplish purposes which are value. They should also know that learning from others who are knowledgeable can enable them to succeed more quickly.

A *guru* is a teacher. A *disciple* is a learner. The purpose of a guru-disciple relationship is to enable disciples to learn how to awaken to their full, spiritual potential. A guru who is spiritually enlightened will not allow an emotionally immature or sentimental, dependent relationship to exist.

Paramahansa Yogananda told his disciples, "I want you to be as [spiritually] strong as I am." Although he interacted with us as a teacher, he also said, "I am not the guru; God is the guru."

What is the relationship between psychological transformation and growing to emotional maturity?

Psychological transformation should result in the removal of conflicts and mental and emotional blockages and promotes orderly growth (development) that culminates in emotional maturity. Emotional maturity along with rational thinking provides a firm foundation for spiritual growth. The spiritual growth of some people is inhibited by their emotional immaturity which contributes to irresponsible behaviors and a tendency to cling to superstitious or erroneous beliefs about God and their relationship with God. People who are emotionally immature often dramatize infantile (childish) attitudes and behaviors.

When one has free time on a weekend, with no work, chores, or other obligations, what is a spiritually useful way to use it?

Enjoy your free time. Be happy. Rest and meditate more. Exercise moderately. Eat lightly. Read to acquire knowledge. Write in a personal journal. Commune with nature. Nurture wholesome relationships. Enjoy the silence.

When possible, schedule a private retreat at least once a month, or as often as you can do it.

How can we learn to sleep superconsciously?

Cultivating superconscious sleep is usually more effective when practiced when we are not too tired or sleepy. Here is one method: Lie on your back, relax, breathe evenly, and drift into a meditative state. Put your attention at the spiritual eye. Mentally chant "Om" at the base chakra, then ascend through the chakras to the spiritual eye, mentally chanting "Om" at each chakra, then to the crown chakra. Pause for a moment, then go down through the chakras, mentally chanting "Om" at each one. Do this a few times. The last time you do it, go down to the heart chakra and maintain awareness from there to the crown chakra. Rest in that calm, relaxed, aware state.

When awake, train yourself to be alert, attentive, and observant. In time, superconscious awareness will always be your normal state.

Do spiritually enlightened people know everything? Are their opinions ever wrong? Do they ever make mistakes?

They have Self- and God-knowledge. They may not know all there is to know about relative events and circumstances unless they direct their attention to them. If they are not well-informed, their opinions may not be any more accurate than the opinions of others and their decisions and actions may not be flawless. Stories are sometimes told about saints who are fluent in any language and who know everything. I have not met such a person, nor have I been provided with any reliable evidence to support such claims.

I am strongly inclined to be devotional. I like ritual and enjoy devotional chanting. Is this a suitable enlightenment path?

Performance of a ritual and devotional chanting can help to focus concentration and elicit a sense of awareness of God. It will be useful to balance your devotional inclination with intellectual inquiry, just as it is useful for individuals who are intellectually inclined to cultivate devotion. Being devotional doesn't mean that we shouldn't use common sense.

Is having a romantic relationship compatible with kriya yoga practice and endeavors to grow spiritually?

It is natural to have and to enjoy a compatible, romantic relationship. An incompatible romantic relationship can cause mental and emotional disturbance, waste energies and other personal resources, and distract attention from matters which are of greater importance. If your romantic relationship is wholesome and compatible, nurture it while being attentive to your duties and your spiritual practices.

Are there any special foods that one who is intent on spiritual growth should eat?

A balanced diet of nutritious foods is recommended. Eat in moderation, sufficient for your needs. Avoid processed foods, especially those which have chemical additives and colorings. According to ayurvedic theory, yogis should include a modest portion of sweet foods which are nourishing—not sugar, but foods that have a sweet after-digestive influence. Maintain your ideal body weight.

I am intent on spiritual growth, but I don't want to become too other worldly or impractical. What do you recommend?

Avoid preoccupation with metaphysical speculation to the extent that you are inclined to be disinterested in relating to, and effectively functioning in, the physical world. Use your improved understanding to skillfully attend to your duties and achieve your worthy goals. Think rationally, be decisive, and enjoy what you do. Some indications that you are progressing on the spiritual path are: needs are more easily provided for; desires are more easily fulfilled; comprehension of metaphysical principles steadily improves; and awareness of the wholeness of life is more vivid.

There is only one realm: the realm of God with a variety of categories, including the physical universe. God can be realized while we are here. Although the physical universe is not our final destination, an understanding of metaphysical (higher) realities makes living in this world easier and enjoyable. Consider practical living as useful training and preparation for what is yet to be accomplished.

When meditating, I don't have exceptional perceptions or feel that I am Self- or God-aware. How can I improve my practice?

Practice a meditation technique, then sit and wait, with your attention and awareness in the front and higher brain. Aspire to be aware without trying to cause anything to occur. Feel that you are meditating *in* God.

At other times, cultivate an alert, attentive mental attitude and peacefully attend to your duties and relationships. Your endeavor to maintain a clear state of awareness when you are not meditating is just as important as meditation practice.

I do not have satisfying results when I meditate. Should I continue to practice? Or is there something else I can do?

Continue to meditate on a regular schedule and learn to enjoy the silent peacefulness. The "something else" to do is to live as skillfully as possible while being aware that you are a spiritual being.

To perceive higher realities, is meditation always necessary?

Such perceptions may result from practice of meditative contemplation, or may occur spontaneously. It is more usual that individuals who know how to meditate are receptive to transcendent perceptions and can more easily sustain them.

This description of a woman's transcendental experience is published in the book *Cosmic Consciousness* (Maurice Bucke, M.D., 1901):

Perfect rest and peace and joy were everywhere, and, more strange than all, there came to me a sense of some serene, magnetic presence — grand and pervading. Presently, what seemed to be a swift, oncoming tidal wave of splendor and glory ineffable came down upon me, and I felt myself enveloped, swallowed up ... I was losing my consciousness, my identity, but was powerless to hold myself. Now came a rapture, so intense that the universe stood still, as if amazed at the unutterable majesty of the spectacle! One, in all the infinite universe! The All-Loving, the Perfect One! The Perfect Wisdom, Truth, Love, and Purity! And with the rapture came the insight. In that same wonderful moment of what might be called supernal bliss, came illumination. I saw with intense inward vision the atoms or molecules, of which seemingly the universe is composed — I know not whether material or spiritual — rearranging themselves, as the cosmos (in its continuous, everlasting life) passes from order to order. What joy when I saw there was no break in the chain—not a link left out—everything in its place and time. Worlds, systems, all blended in one harmonious whole.

Paramahansa Yogananda described an early experience of cosmic consciousness in a poem:

Knowing, Knower, Known, as One!
Tranquil, unbroken thrill, eternally living,
      ever-new peace.
Enjoyable beyond imagination and expectancy,
      samadhi bliss!
Not an unconscious state
Or mental chloroform without willful return,
Samadhi but extends my conscious realm
Beyond the limits of the mortal frame
To the farthest boundary of eternity
Where I, the Cosmic Sea,
Watch the little ego floating in Me.

The 16th century Spanish mystic John Yepes (St. John of the Cross) described an experience that occurred when he was absorbed in intensive, prayerful contemplation:

After some time, certain rays of light, comfort, and divine sweetness scattered these mists and translated the soul of the servant of God into a paradise of inner delights and heavenly sweetness. This sovereign wisdom is of an excellence so high that no faculty or science can unto it attain.

Many people who have had such experiences say that they perceived the order, harmony and goodness of life, were inspired to live with renewed interest, and no longer feared death. They did not feel special or superior to others.

Some individuals had only one such experience. Others, knowing how to calm the mind and be receptive, were able to have similar insights that enlarged their understanding and enabled them to integrate their realizations into everyday life.

*Is there a relationship between subjective perceptions and pro-
cesses that occur in the brain?*

The brain interprets sensory impulses, coordinates and regulates bodily functions, and processes thoughts, emotions, and
awareness. A typical adult human brain weighs about three
pounds, contains 100 billion nerve cells, consumes 25 percent of
the body's oxygen, and uses most of the body's calories. The
nervous system consists of the brain, spinal cord, nerves, and
ganglia (nerve cells outside the brain and spinal cord), and coordinates and regulates internal functions of the body and responses
to external stimuli.

The sympathetic nervous system depresses secretions, de-
creases smooth muscle tone, and contracts vascular systems
(vessels through which fluids circulate). It regulates physical
characteristics associated with arousal and action—the "flight
or fight response" related to survival behaviors.

The parasympathetic nervous system, originating in the central and back regions of the brain and lower spinal cord, regulates the digestive system, slows the heart, dilates blood vessels,
and has a quieting influence.

Neurotheology (*neuro*, nerve; *theology*, study of God and religious experience) is a word used by modern researchers who
attempt to discover what occurs in the brain and nervous system
when a person perceives a reality that is different and seems
more meaningful than ordinary experiences. Data obtained from
individuals who pray and meditate to a "peak experience" level
of awareness enables researchers to relate subjective states of
awareness to specific regions of the brain.

The prefrontal lobes of the brain are involved when attention
is concentrated. This is one reason why practitioners of yogic
meditative contemplation are advised to direct their attention to
the front region of the brain when they meditate.

The "orientation association centers" in the upper, back region of both hemispheres of the brain process perceptions of our
sense of relationship to space, time, and the external environ-

ment. If sensory input is blocked to this region, the brain is prevented from forming a distinction between "self" and "nonself." When the left orientation center cannot find any boundary between the sense of self and the world, the self is perceived as being one with everything. When the right orientation center is quiet, a sense that only infinite space exists is experienced.

A weak magnetic field placed near the left temporal lobe of the brain caused some individuals to have a sensation of a "presence" that is often described as benevolent or divine. Sensory deprivation, lack of oxygen, insufficient sleep, extreme tiredness, chanting, singing, a severe personal crisis, participation in religious ceremonies, prayer, and meditation can produce altered states of consciousness.

Even though what seem to be "spiritual experiences" may be associated with neural stimulation (or lack of it), it should not be too quickly presumed that all such episodes are mind or brain-produced phenomena.

Authentic spiritual perceptions and emergence of innate knowledge regarding our real nature and our relationship with the Infinite always contribute to mental health, diminishment of ego-sense, and a keen interest in living. Disordered mental states and hallucinations may result in confusion, an inflated sense of self-importance, or lack of interest in living.

You are in this world for but a little while. The ultimate purpose for being here is much different than what most people imagine it to be. If you want divine guidance in your life, don't waste time in idle talk. Silence is the altar of Spirit. – *Paramahansa Yogananda*

Glossary

absolute Perfect, complete. Pure, not mixed. Not limited.

actualize To realize in action. Abilities are actualized when they are expressed. Goals are actualized when they are accomplished.

affirm Latin *affirmare*, to strengthen. To declare to be true.

agnosticism The theory that, while not denying the existence of God, asserts that God cannot be known; that only objective phenomena are objects of real knowledge.

astral realm The field of life forces and energies.

atheism Disbelief in or denial of the existence of God.

avatar The emergence of divine qualities and powers in human form. A spiritually enlightened soul that incarnates to impart divine influences into planetary consciousness. The "universal avatar" concept is that divine qualities are unveiled and become increasingly influential as individual and collective consciousness becomes illumined.

awareness Our awareness reflects perceptions to our mind and consciousness.

ayurveda Sanskrit *ayus*, life; *veda*, knowledge. A natural way to nurture total well-being that evolved in India thousands of years ago. Diagnostic procedures include examination of the patient's pulse, body temperature, skin, eyes, psychological characteristics, behaviors, and other factors. Treatment includes recommended foods and herbs for specific purposes, attitude adjustment, behavior modification, detoxification regimens, meditation practice, and other procedures used to restore balance to the basic mind-body constitution.

One's basic mind-body constitution is regulated by three *doshas* or subtle governing principles (*vata*, space-air; *pitta*, fire; *kapha*, water-earth). Foods are recommended according to their taste-influences (sweet, sour, salty, pungent, bitter, astringent) on the doshas. Food transformation is said to progress through seven stages: plasma, blood, muscle, fat, bone, bone marrow, and reproductive essences.

In the *Charaka Samhita*, a primary ayurvedic text, medicinal uses of more than five hundred herbs are described. Knowledge of ayurveda flowed from India to Tibet, China, and Mediterranean countries, and more recently to Europe and the Americas. During the years of British rule in India, ayurvedic practices declined in urban areas but continued to be the health treatment of choice among rural populations. Several ayurvedic colleges in India have been established in recent years and many clinics in other countries are providing ayurvedic services.

Siddha medicine, a similar wellness system, evolved in south India. Its many texts are said to have been written by enlightened saints, among whom Agastya is especially revered. Practitioners of this system also prescribe the ashes of gems and purified metals for healing and physical rejuvenation.

Bhagavad Gita Holy or divine song (*bhaj*, to revere or love, *gai*, song). An allegoric literary work in which Krishna (representing enlightened consciousness) is portrayed as an avatar teaching his disciple-friend Arjuna "the eternal way of righteousness" with emphasis on knowledge, selfless service, devotion, and meditation.

bliss The sheer joy of awareness of pure being rather than only a happy mental state or an emotional feeling or mood.

buddhi From the Sanskrit verb-root *budh* to know. A fully, spiritually aware person is said to be a buddha. Because souls are units of one Reality, all have a pure conscious or "buddha nature."

capacity The ability to receive, hold, or absorb.

causal realm The field of cosmic, electrical, and magnetic forces emanated from the field of primordial nature.

chakra Sanskrit "wheel." Any of the seven, subtle vital centers in the spine and brain, each with unique attributes.

The first chakra at the base of the spine has the earth element attribute. The prana frequency taste is sweet. The color is yellow. The sound is as restless buzzing of bees. Sanskrit *muladhara*, "foundation." A characteristic of this chakra is stability.

Second chakra: at the sacrum of the spine. Water element. The taste is astringent. The color is white. The sound is like that of a flute. Sanskrit *swadhisthana*, "abode of ordinary self-consciousness." A characteristic influence is sensualness.

Third chakra: at the lumbar region of the spine opposite the navel. Fire-element. The taste is bitter. The color is red. The sound is like that of a harp. Sanskrit *manipura*, "the city of jewels." When awareness is identified here, one may express self-control and fervent aspiration to spiritual growth.

Fourth chakra: at the dorsal region of the spine between the shoulder blades. Air element. The taste is sour. The color is blue. The sound is like a continuous peal of a gong. Sanskrit *anahata*, "unstruck sound." When awareness is identified here, one may have mastery of the senses and life forces.

Fifth chakra: at the cervical region of the spine, opposite the throat. Ether (space) element. The taste is pungent. The color is gray or misty with sparkling pinpoints of white light. The sound is like the roar of the ocean. Sanskrit *vishudda*, "pure." When awareness is identified here, one may have exceptional powers of intellectual and intuitive discernment.

Sixth chakra: Between the eyebrows, associated with the front lobes of the brain. Life forces flowing upward and focused here may be perceived as a dark blue orb with a golden halo centered with a silver-white light. Gold is said to be the life force frequency of Om; dark blue, the frequency of all-pervading Consciousness; the white starlike light has all of the colors of the spectrum. Sanskrit *ajna*, "command."

Seventh chakra: Related, but not confined, to the higher brain. Pure consciousness. Transcendence of mental and physical states and of all conditions that modify or distort awareness. Sanskrit *sahasrara*, "thousand rayed."

compassion Empathetic concern for the suffering or misfortune of others together with an inclination to give aid or support.

concentration An undisturbed flow of attention.

consciousness In ordinary usage: our awareness of self-identity and the totality of feelings, attitudes, opinions, beliefs, what we know to be true, and the quality and degree of our tendencies and capacities to be influenced by external conditions and be either reactive or responsive to them.

contemplate Latin *com*, intensive; *templum*, space for observing something. To ponder or to consider as being possible. To hopefully look at with expectation.

cosmic consciousness Awareness of the unified wholeness of life.

Cosmic Mind The one Universal Mind of which particularized minds are units or parts. Our mental states, subliminal tendencies and urges, thoughts, desires, and intentions interact with Cosmic Mind which is inclined to respond by manifesting corresponding circumstances.

decisive Characterized by determined or resolute choice.

deism The belief that God created the universe, but is apart from it, has no influence on phenomena, and provides no revelation.

delusion An erroneous idea or belief.

devotion Strong attraction. Attachment or loyalty.

dharma The influence that upholds and supports the universe and living things and empowers evolution. Dharmic living is living that is in harmony with the cosmic order. To adhere to one's path in life in accord with the orderly processes of nature is to fulfill one's dharma: purposes that are constructive and meaningful.

disciple Latin *discipulus*; from *discere*, to learn. An adherent of a philosophical system or spiritual tradition.

ego The soul's illusional sense of selfhood that causes and sustains a mistaken sense of self-identity. When the ego is purified, one is aware of being an individualized unit of infinite Consciousness.

egotism An exaggerated sense of self importance; arrogance.

elicit To bring forth.

emotion A subjective feeling-response to something: compassion, love (attraction), aversion, fear, revulsion, elation, or any other feeling-response that one might have.

enlightenment To provide with insight and/or spiritual wisdom.

era A duration of time. See *yuga*.

ether Space with fine cosmic forces with potential to form as matter. The other four subtle element-influences are air (gas), fire, water, and earth which interact to express as corresponding material manifestations. The five subtle element-influences are the true essences of the manifest universe. Material manifestation of the elements is said to occur when one half of one subtle element-influence combines with an eighth of a part of each of the other four subtle element-influences.

field An area in which events can occur. Our awareness is a field. Cosmic Mind is a field. The Oversoul aspect of Consciousness and the realm of primordial nature are fields. Physics: a region of space indicated by physical properties such as gravitational or electromagnetic forces.

God The absolute aspect is existence-being. The expressive aspect (Godhead or Oversoul) has attributes which pervade its emanated, vibrating power (Om).

The word *god* has been traced via Germanic to an Indo-European language in which an ancestor form means "the invoked one." The surviving non-Germanic relative is Sanskrit *hu* (invoke the Gods), a form of which is in the Rig-Veda (Hymn of Knowledge), an ancient Hindu scripture: *puru-hutas* (much invoked), characterizes an aspect of cosmic power depicted as the ruler of thunder and lightning. The Sanskrit word Brahma is used to refer to the expanding, creation-producing aspect of God. The absolute aspect is referred to as Brahman.

Muslims, adherents of Islam devoted to the ideal of submission to God, use the word Allah (al-Lah), The Great Adored. Christians use the words God, Heavenly Father, and Lord.

Names that are used to refer to God (Old English, the Highest Good) reflect what people imagined as the highest attribute of deity. Zoroastrians (in ancient Persia, now Iran) used Ahura Mazda, The Wise Creator. In Hinduism, some aspects of deity are characterized according to their presumed influences or roles: Divine Mother, nurturing influence; Ishwara, ruler; Shiva, the transformative, regenerative influence; Vishnu, that which preserves; Saraswati, goddess of speech and learning; Lakshmi, goddess of prosperity and good fortune. Goddesses are depicted as the creative energies of the gods, the cosmic forces and their unique influences.

Godhead   The Oversoul aspect of supreme Consciousness. The first self-manifested aspect which emanates vibrating power (Om) that produces and sustains universes.

grace   Freely given benefits, good fortune, provision or support.

guna   A constituent attribute of Consciousness that pervades creation and regulates its cosmic forces. The influences of the three attributes are described as 1) *sattwic*, elevating and illuminating; 2) *rajasic*, transformative; 3) *tamasic*, inertial.

guru   That which removes darkness. A teacher. In enlightenment traditions a guru is viewed as a conduit through which higher knowledge and transformative spiritual force can be transmitted to receptive disciples. Yogic teachings are authentic and transformative when they are transmitted through a lineage of enlightened gurus. The gurus of the kriya yoga lineage that I represent are as follows:

Mahavatar Babaji. Little is known of this spiritual master who is in seclusion in the Himalayas. Paramahansa Yogananda often referred to him as a *maha* (great) *avatar* (embodiment of divine qualities) and wrote about him in his book *Autobiography of a Yogi*. *Baba* (father) is a descriptive word commonly used in India when speaking about a man whose characteristics are considered to be exceptional. The suffix "ji" is used to indicate reverent respect. Babaji revived and vitalized the ancient teachings and spiritual practices of kriya yoga which had become almost forgotten during a previous Dark Age.

Shyama Charan Lahiri (September 30, 1828–1895), a disciple of Mahavatar Babaji. The title *Mahasaya* (one who is large-minded or cosmic conscious) was used by his disciples. Married, the father of three sons and two daughters, he lived in Banaras now Varanasi) and was employed in government service. His free time was used for meditation and instructing disciples (more than five thousand) in the practices of kriya yoga.

Swami Sri Yukteswar (May 20, 1855–March 9, 1936), a disciple of Lahiri Mahasaya. Named Priya Nath Karar when he was born, he was ordained into the monastic order of swamis several years after his wife died. An master of yoga, Sri Yukteswar was respected for his intellectual powers and knowledge of Vedic scriptures.

Paramahansa Yogananda (January 5, 1893–March 7, 1952). His family name was Mukunda Lal Ghosh. Yogananda (God-union bliss) was the monastic name by which he became widely known after he was ordained into the swami order by Sri Yukteswar—who later gave him the further title of Paramahansa (one who is firmly established in transcendental consciousness).

I was initiated by Paramahansa Yogananda in 1950 and was ordained by him in late 1951, in Los Angeles, California.

hallucination A false or distorted perception of objects or events with a vivid sense of their being real. Mind-produced phenomena which does not have any real basis.

heart The physical heart is a hollow, muscular organ that pumps blood. The metaphysical meaning is the essence of one's being.

holistic Emphasizing the importance of the wholeness of something and the interdependence of its parts and processes.

humility Absence of egotism.

illusion Latin *illusio*, an imitation or counterfeit of something. A mistaken perception of subjective or objective reality: of thoughts, concepts, feelings, or external things or events.

imagination A mental picture or concept of something which does not yet exist or does not exist in the present environment. Fantasy is unregulated imagination.

initiation Latin *initium*, beginning; from *inire*, to go in. A new beginning. A rite of passage into a body of knowledge and the company of adherents of that knowledge.

inspire Latin *inspirare*: *in-*, into, and *spirare*, to breath. To be inspired is to be guided, affected, or aroused by divine influence.

intellect The faculty of discrimination or discernment.

intuition Direct perception without the aid of the senses.

karma An influence that can cause effects to occur. Accumulated mental conditionings and influential subliminal tendencies and urges comprise one's personal karmic condition (which is of the mind, not of the true Self).

kundalini Soul force. In people who are not yet spiritually awake, it is mostly dormant. In spiritually awake people, its energies are active, transformative, and empowering. They are aroused by aspiration to spiritual growth, devotion, meditation and other practices, being in places where spiritual forces are strong, and mental and spiritual attunement with an enlightened person.

life 1. The property or quality manifested in growth, metabolism, response to stimuli, and reproduction. 2. The physical, mental, and spiritual experiences that make up our sense of existence.

light Electromagnetic radiation. Light travels at 186,000 miles per second. The sun's radiation travels 93 million miles in almost 8 minutes to our planet where we perceive some of it as visible light when it impacts earth's magnetic field.

mantra From Sanskrit *manas*, mind, and *tra*, to protect. A word, word-phrase, or sound used to focus attention when meditating.

material A substance of which something is made.

matter Something that occupies space. Matter is confined energy.

maya That which measures, defines, limits, and produces forms of matter. A characteristic of the primordial field of nature.

meditation An undisturbed flow of attention to an object or ideal to be identified with or realized. Intentional detachment of attention and awareness from external conditions, the senses, emotions, and mental states that enables one to realize the pure-conscious essence of being and the reality of God.

metaphysics Latin *metaphysica* < Greek *tà metà tà physikà*, "the things after the physics," the title of Aristotle's treatise on first principles, so-called because it followed his work on physics. The branch of philosophy that investigates the nature of first principles of ultimate reality, including the nature of being and cosmology.

mind Sanskrit *manas*, to think; hence *man*, thinker. The faculty that processes perceptions and information.

modify To change the character of something. To limit or restrict. Our ordinary awareness is modified by acquired information, erroneous opinions, misperceptions of facts, sleep, and memories. Superconsciousness is unmodified.

mysticism Spiritual discipline practiced to experience unification of one's attention and awareness with God or ultimate reality by contemplative meditation. The experience of such realization. Belief in the existence of realities beyond ordinary powers of perception which are accessible by subjective experience, as by intuition.

nadi A channel or pathway through which prana (life force) flows. *Ida nadi* is the left channel along the spine, the lunar influence. *Pingala* is the right channel, the solar influence. *Sushumna nadi*, the central channel, is the path through which vital forces ascend when attention is internalized or when certain meditation methods (such as kriya pranayama) are used. Within sushumna nadi are two astral channels and a fine channel of consciousness-matter.

ojas A refined energy that strengthens the body's immune system and energizes the mind. The final product of food transformation. It is increased by managing stress, conservation and transmutation of physical and mental forces, mental and emotional calmness, wholesome living, spiritual practices, and cultivation of superconsciousness.

Om The vibration of the power of Consciousness.

omnipotence Unlimited power.

omnipresence Present everywhere.

omniscience All knowing.

Oversoul See *Godhead*.

philosophy Latin *philosophia*, from Greek *philosophos*. The love and seeking of wisdom by diligent inquiry and moral self-discipline.

prana Life force. Its aspects influence specific life-support systems. Soul force flows into the body at the medulla oblongata at the base of the brain. When prana flows freely, health prevails. When flows of prana are imbalanced, weak, or disturbed, psychological and physical discomfort or distress may occur. Pranayama practice harmonizes flows of prana in the body and allows its expansion.

pranayama Sanskrit *pran(a)*, life force; *ayama*, not restrained. The formal practice of pranayama usually involves regulation of breathing rhythms to harmonize flows of life force in the body and calm the mind as preparation for meditation practice.

primordial nature The first field of cosmic manifestation in which Om and Om's self-manifested aspects—space, time, and cosmic forces— are unified.

prosperity Having success, thriving. When the spiritual, mental, emotional, physical, and environmental components of our lives are harmoniously integrated, we are truly prosperous.

psyche In Western cultures the psyche (Latin from Greek *psykhe*, soul) is usually viewed as "the mind functioning as the center of thought, feeling, and behavior and consciously or unconsciously adjusting and relating the body to its social and physical environment." A soul (the original meaning of the word) in one part of the world is not different from other souls. How people view themselves in relationship to God and the world and how they think and act are often different.

The practical means by which obstacles to spiritual growth can be removed are the same and can be used by everyone. When first learning about spiritual practices that evolved in other regions of the world, some people have difficulty grasping new philosophical concepts or the words used to describe them. Or they may falsely presume that cultural behaviors unlike their own must be adopted. Acquired mental attitudes and habits may also be a problem: in cultures where self-reliance and a strong sense of individualism is emphasized, resistance to having a teacher or to purifying the ego may be obstacles to learning and spiritual growth.

realization Comprehension, to experience and know.

redemptive The capacity to restore, rescue, free, or liberate.

reincarnation The return of souls to physical embodiment because of necessity or the soul's inclination to have experiences here. It is not spiritually beneficial to be overly concerned about possible, previous, or future earth-sojourns. Our attention and endeavors should instead be focused on authentic spiritual growth that will result in liberation of consciousness.

renunciation The letting go of mental and emotional attachments to things, circumstances, emotional states, memories, actions and the results of actions while being involved in meaningful activities and relationships.

sage A wise person.

saint A person whose divine qualities are expressive.

salvation A condition of freedom from pain or discomfort, which may be temporary or permanent in accord with one's degree of Self- and God-realization.

samadhi "To bring together completely." Preliminary samadhi is supported by objects of perception. Higher, pure samadhi is devoid of perceived objects.

science Disciplined observation, identification, and experimental investigation of mundane phenomena or of higher realities.

seer One who clearly sees (discerns) the truth of what is observed.

Self An individualized unit of pure consciousness; the core essence of being. Our true nature, rather the illusional sense of selfhood (ordinary, egocentric self-consciousness). When identified with matter and a mind or body the Self is referred to as a soul. Units of pure consciousness are individualized when interactions between the life-essence of God and primordial nature interact with the primordial field of nature. Self-realization is actualized when the difference between one's pure essence of being and ordinary awareness is discerned.

soul See *Self*.

space The infinite extension of three-dimensional reality in which events occur.

spiritual Of or related to God and souls.

spiritual eye The sixth chakra, located in the forehead between and above the eyebrows. Light may be perceived here when a meditator's attention is focused and the mind is calm. See *chakra*.

stage A level, degree, or period of time in the course of a process.

subjective Existing only in one's mind or awareness.

subliminal Below the threshold of conscious awareness. Subliminal drives and tendencies activate thoughts and emotions. When they are pacified, the mind is calm and awareness is clear.

superconscious Latin *super*, above, over. Superconscious states are superior to ordinary states of consciousness.

technique A systematic procedure. A meditation technique can be used to elicit relaxation, calm the mind, and focus attention.

time An interval between events. A part of a continuum (wholeness) which includes space and cosmic forces, no part of which can be distinguished from the others except by arbitrary (individual judgment) division for the purpose of analysis or theoretical speculation.

Our concept of time is related to things and events: pendulums swing; quartz crystals vibrate; atoms, light waves, electric and magnetic fields and planets move. But what is time like in a void where nothing exists? In an absolute void only the Something that makes relative happenings possible exists.

The interval of time we call a year marks one revolution of the earth around the sun; a day is one spin of the earth around its axis; a month was once related to the duration of the orbit of the moon. Astronomical measures of time are not absolute. The moon is farther away from the earth than it was many thousands of years ago. Five hundred million years ago, a day was about twenty hours long. Days and years are variable happenings rather than exact markings of time. Our seven-day week is arbitrary. Through the ages, various cultures have had five day, eight day, and ten day weeks.

Until the fourteenth century, days were divided into irregular intervals of morning, noon, evening, and night. Summer daylight hours are longer than winter daylight hours. Hours and minutes and time zones began to be standardized only a few centuries ago.

At the Equator, the earth's rate of spin is 1000 miles an hour. Its speed around the sun is almost 20 miles a second (72,000 miles an hour). Our solar system in relationship to the center of our galaxy is moving at the rate of 120 miles a second (432,000 miles an hour). Our galaxy is moving toward another galaxy (Andromeda) at 50 miles a second (180,000 miles an hour).

Time need not be thought of as an insurmountable obstacle to spiritual growth. Refinements of the nervous system, however, and other physical changes that may be necessary to accommodate higher states of consciousness, occur in time.

transcendental Rising above common thoughts, ideas, or states of consciousness. Interest in the underlying basis of knowledge.

Transcendental Field Absolute or pure Consciousness. Referred to as existence-being because it does not have attributes. The ultimate stage of God-realization.

veda Knowledge.

Vedas The oldest known religious scriptures that emerged in India more than five thousand years ago. The teaching emphasis is that one Reality exists and can be known.

wisdom The understanding of what is true, right, or enduring.

yoga Sanskrit *yug*, to yoke or unify. 1. Samadhi, the meaning used in Patanjali's yoga-sutras. 2. Practice that enable a person to be Self- and God-realized.

Hatha Yoga: movements and postures (*asanas*) that strengthen the body and contribute to overall health and well-being; procedures used to acquire control over involuntary physical functions and awaken kundalini energies; pranayama; and meditation practice.

Bhakti Yoga: the way of love, compassion, devotion to God, and reverence for life.

Karma Yoga: the way of constructive, selfless action.

Jnana (gyana) Yoga: the way of acquiring higher knowledge by using powers of discriminative intelligence and intuition.

Raja (superior) Yoga: described in chapter two of this book.

Kriya Yoga includes the useful practices of all of the yogic systems.

yuga An era or designated duration of time. Many centuries ago, Vedic astronomer-seers taught a theory of time-cycles to explain the effects of cosmic forces on human beings and the trends of evolution that affect Planet Earth.

An ascending cycle is half of a complete 24,000 year cycle:

- 1,200 years of a Dark Age of confusion during which most people are intellectually deficient and spiritually unaware.
- 2,400 years of a second era during which the intellectual powers and spiritual awareness of people increase and electric and magnetic properties of nature are known and used. We are now 300 years into a 2,400-year ascending cycle, which will continue until 4,100.
- 3,600 years of a third era during which mental powers are highly developed.
- 4,800 years of a fourth era during which most of the people on our planet are spiritually conscious.

This calculation of time-cycles, first published by Paramahansa Yogananda's guru Sri Yukteswar in 1895, is based on the theory that forces from the center of our galaxy influence the electromagnetic field of the solar system and the mental and intellectual faculties of its human inhabitants.

When our solar system is most distant from the galactic center, human mental and intellectual powers are weak, soul awareness is obscured, and inability to comprehend the facts of life is common. When our sun is nearest to the galactic center, intellectual and intuitive powers are highly developed.

Because a mistake was made (circa 700 B.C.E.) in calculating the progression of time-cycles, many people still erroneously believe that we are in a Dark Age of confusion.

Individual truth seekers need not be confined by external events. Because of their intensive spiritual practice they can awaken from a condition of mental confusion, develop their intellectual, mental, and intuitive powers, and be spiritually enlightened.